To Eddie Kantar, a great author and teacher. His wit, style and presence have helped students and instructors alike, all over the world, to learn and teach this wonderful game.

Barbara Seagram
David Bird

BARBARA SEAGRAM & DAVID BIRD

BRIDGE

25 WAYS TO BE A BETTER DEFENDER

MASTER POINT PRESS • TORONTO

Master Point Press
331 Douglas Ave.
Toronto, Ontario, Canada
M5M 1H2
(416) 781-0351
Website: http://www.masterpointpress.com
Email: info@masterpointpress.com

Library and Archives Canada Cataloguing in Publication

Seagram, Barbara
    Bridge : 25 ways to be a better defender / written by Barbara Seagram & David Bird.

ISBN 1-897106-11-4
ISBN 978-1-897106-11-2

1. Contract bridge--Defensive play. I. Bird, David, 1946- II. Title.

GV1282.42.S39 2006   796.41'53   C2006-902112-0

We acknowledge the financial support of the Government of Canada through the Book Publishing Industry Development Program (BPIDP) for our publishing activities.

Editor	Ray Lee
Cover and interior design	Olena S. Sullivan/New Mediatrix
Interior format	Luise Lee
Copyediting	Suzanne Hocking

Printed in Canada by Webcom

3 4 5 6 7   14 13 12 11 10

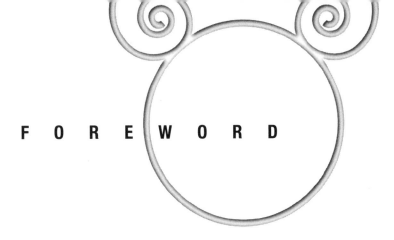

F O R E W O R D

Suppose someone said to you, "Close your eyes and picture a great bridge champion at the table." What image would come to mind? Jeff Meckstroth studying his cards, deciding whether to bid a slam? Bob Hamman deep in thought, deciding how to play a tricky 3NT? If your answer is one of these, we'll believe you. It is very unlikely that you would imagine anyone defending a contract, because for some reason this is a neglected aspect of the game. It is not thought to be glamorous, even though finding the only defense to beat a contract is one of the most satisfying parts of the game.

Many average players go through their bridge careers making the same defensive mistakes time and again. They give away countless tricks by covering an honor when they shouldn't or playing high in the third seat when it is necessary to play a lower card. In this book we cover all the situations where it is easy to go wrong. The first section, The Basics of Sound Defense, covers such topics as opening leads, correct play in the second and third seats, whether you should defend actively or passively and how to preserve communications with your partner. The second section, Building a Picture of the Hidden Hands, shows you how to discover what cards declarer and your partner hold. With all the cards known, defense becomes so much easier! Finally, in the third section, we cover some more advanced topics, such as how you can put declarer to a guess, promoting trump tricks, disrupting declarer's communications and defending deceptively.

If you are new to the game, you may think that we have given you a mountain to climb. Don't worry. There are twenty-five chapters and you can tackle them one at a time, at your own pace. Each chapter you absorb will make you a better defender. Your partners will notice the difference. If they don't, then lend them this book! Good luck.

Barbara Seagram and David Bird

C O N T E N T S

THE BASICS OF
SOUND DEFENSE

CHAPTER

LEADS, SIGNALS AND DISCARDS

 If one does not know to which port one is sailing, no wind is favorable.
Seneca

Any book on defense needs to lay out, right at the start, the basic methods that will be assumed throughout. Are we going to suggest something new and wonderful? No! You will be relieved to hear that we are going to recommend methods that have been tried and tested over the decades.

Opening leads

We will look first at opening leads. In later chapters we will explain how you should choose which suit to lead. Sometimes it is right to attack by trying to score tricks or set them up. Other times it is better to be passive, seeking an opening lead that is unlikely to give a trick away. For the moment, we will consider only the particular card that you should lead from various suit holdings. The choice of card is usually the same, whether you are defending a suit contract or a notrump contract.

Which card should I lead against notrump?

✦ From a 'perfect sequence' of three or more honors, lead the top card: the ace from A-K-Q; the king from K-Q-J.

✦ From a 'broken sequence' of three or more honors, again lead the top card: the ace from A-K-J; the queen from Q-J-9.

✦ From an interior sequence, lead the top of the touching honors: the jack from K-J-10; the ten from Q-10-9.

✦ From a holding of four or more cards containing at least one honor (not a sequence of three), lead the fourth-best card: the two from K-8-7-2 and the four from Q-J-6-4-3.

✦ From a holding of three cards containing one honor or two non-touching honors, lead the bottom card: the five from Q-8-5; the three from K-J-3.

✦ From three cards containing touching honors, lead the top honor: the king from K-Q-4; the jack from J-10-5.

✦ Lead the top card from a doubleton.

What should I lead from three or four small cards?

Suppose you decide to make a lead from ♥8-5-2. Which card should you lead? We recommend 'top of nothing' from three small cards. When partner sees your ♥8, he will know that you are leading from weakness. Many players in Europe lead the second-best card from a weak suit and would lead the ♥5; however, it then becomes difficult to distinguish between ♥K-8-5 and ♥8-5-2. Some players in North America lead the ♥2 from ♥8-5-2, but this makes it impossible to tell if they are leading from strength or weakness. You won't go far wrong by leading 'top of nothing'.

The situation is slightly different when you hold four cards. Now the lead of your top card may cost a trick. Suppose you are West here:

```
                ♠ Q 5 3
  ♠ 9 7 6 2   [          ]   ♠ J 10
                ♠ A K 8 4
```

If you lead a top-of-nothing ♠9, declarer will make four tricks in the suit, scoring the ♠8 on the fourth round. It is better to lead the second-best card from four small, preserving your top card. Lead the ♠7 and you will restrict declarer to three tricks in the suit.

You get the idea, then. You lead a low spot card to suggest that you have something good in the suit and would welcome it being continued. A high spot card suggests that you are leading from a weak suit and it may be a good idea for partner to look elsewhere for tricks when he gains the lead.

Do I lead the same card against a suit contract?

Most of the time you choose the same card from a given combination, whether you are leading against a suit contract or a contract in notrump. There are two exceptions to this rule. Suppose you hold ♠A-10-8-6-3. The ♠6 is a promising lead against a notrump contract, because you hope to set up the suit and score several spade tricks later, whereas the ♠6 would be a very poor lead against a suit contract. If declarer had a singleton spade, in his own hand or the dummy, you might never make a trick with your ace! Almost certainly, you would do better to lead a different suit. If you are determined to lead a spade, you must lead the ace.

Do not underlead an ace against a suit contract

Suppose next that you hold ♥K-Q-8-5-2. The ♥5 would make an admirable lead against a notrump contract because you hope to set up the suit and score several heart tricks later. However, there is little possibility of doing this against a suit contract because someone will be able to ruff the third round. If you choose to lead from this combination against a suit contract, you must lead the ♥K. Even if declarer wins with the ♥A, which you rather expect, you can score the ♥Q on the second round.

Lead the higher of touching honors against a suit contract

How do I tell partner that I like his lead?

When partner leads a low card, you will often have to play 'third hand high' in an attempt to win the trick or force declarer to win with a higher card, thereby promoting a trick for the defense. When instead partner leads an honor, you may have a choice of spot cards to play and a chance to 'signal'. What does this mean? You choose one of your spot cards to pass a message to your partner. The most popular scheme of signaling is to play a high card to indicate that you like the suit and would welcome a continuation; a low card discourages a continuation. This is known as giving an 'attitude signal'. Here is a straightforward example:

	♠ 8 6 5	
♠ A K 10 3	□	♠ Q 9 2
	♠ J 7 4	

West, your partner, leads the ♠A against a contract of four hearts. You expect him to hold the ♠K as well (because it is usually a bad idea to lead an ace when you do not also hold the king). Since you hold the ♠Q, you want to encourage the opening lead. You follow with the ♠9 on the first round. Noting your encouraging signal, West continues with the ♠K and then a low spade, allowing you to score three tricks in the suit.

Now suppose that the spade layout had been different:

♠ 8 6 5

♠ A K 10 3   ▭   ♠ J 9 2

♠ Q 7 4

Again your partner leads the ♠A against a heart contract. This time you do not want partner to continue the suit, because you fear that it will set up South's ♠Q. You therefore follow with your lowest spot card, the ♠2, giving a discouraging signal. West will switch to a different suit and you will avoid giving declarer an undeserved spade trick. (If West held ♠A-K-Q he would continue the suit anyway, of course. Your signal simply shows him what you hold. It is not a command to do one thing or another.)

Is it different when declarer leads a suit?

The situation changes when declarer leads a suit. This will usually be a suit where he holds most of the strength — a suit that he is trying to establish. There is no point in telling partner whether you want the suit to be continued or not. (Declarer is playing the suit, anyway!) Instead you should use your signal for a different purpose, to let your partner know how many cards you hold in the suit. This is known as 'giving a count signal'. A high spot card shows an even number of cards in the suit. A low spot card shows an odd number of cards.

Why should partner be interested in how many cards you hold in a suit? Because he can then work out many cards declarer has. It will also help him to build a 'complete count of the hand' — in other words to determine the shape of each player's hand. The more you play bridge, the more you will appreciate how important it is to count the shape of the hands.

A direct benefit of count signals may arise when one of the defenders has the chance to disrupt declarer's communications by holding up an ace. Suppose declarer leads the ♦8 from his hand here:

♦ K Q J 10 4

♦ 9 6 2   ▭   ♦ A 5 3

♦ 8 7

Sitting West, you follow with the ♦2. This is a count signal, a low spot card showing that you have an odd number of cards in the suit. From East's point of view it is likely that you hold three diamonds, leaving declarer with two. He will therefore refuse to take the ♦A until the second round, aiming to cut declarer's communications to the remaining diamond winners. (If the ♦2 happens to be a singleton, with declarer holding four diamonds, it will not matter when East takes his ♦A.)

What is a 'high' spot card?

BY THE WAY

When you signal with your spot cards by playing first a high one and then a lower one, this is called an 'echo'. It is used to signal either encouragement or an even number of cards, depending on who is leading the suit. In the U.K. the same signal is called a 'peter', an old whist term derived from the Blue Peter, a flag that is hoisted when a ship is ready to sail.

Sometimes you hear players say, "We treat the seven or above as a high card; six or below is treated as a low card." There is not much sense in that! You can only signal with the cards that you hold in your hand.

Suppose partner has led the ♠A and you want to signal encouragement from your ♠Q-3-2. The best you can do is follow with the ♠3. A watchful partner will note that the ♠2 is 'missing'. He may therefore conclude that you intend your ♠3 as an encouraging card.

Now imagine that partner has led the ♠A and you want to discourage from ♠J-9-7. The best you can do is signal with the ♠7. Partner should take a close look at all the spot cards in his own hand and the dummy, as well as the card that declarer has played. He will often be able to deduce that your ♠7 is a discouraging card.

Discards

When declarer (or your partner) leads a suit in which you hold no more cards, you have the opportunity to pass a message to your partner with your choice of discard. The most popular and traditional scheme is that a high card shows interest in the suit that you discard; a low card shows disinterest. So, you might discard the ♣9 from ♣K-Q-9-8-2 to tell partner that you hold strong clubs. From ♥10-8-7-6-3 you would discard the ♥3 to indicate a lack of interest in the suit. We will return to the important topic of discarding in two later chapters.

Summary

✔ Once you have chosen which suit to lead, the choice of card from within that suit is usually a matter of convention (for example, fourth best from a suit containing an honor).

✔ Throughout the book, assume the use of the lead conventions that we recommend at the start of this introductory chapter (p. 12).

✔ When *partner leads to a trick* and you have the opportunity to signal, play a high card to encourage that suit or a low card to discourage. This is known as an *attitude signal.*

✔ When *declarer leads to a trick* and you have the opportunity to signal, play a high card to show an even number of cards in the suit or a low card to show an odd number. This is a *count signal.*

✔ When you are discarding, a high card shows that you like that suit; a low card shows that you have no interest there.

✔ All signals and discards are intended to show what you hold, rather than to tell partner what to do. Your partner will look at all the evidence available, including the cards in his own hand, before deciding on the best line of defense.

LEADS, SIGNALS AND DISCARDS

NOW TRY THESE...

1. What card would you lead from the following holdings against a contract of 3NT?

   - (a) ♠ A 9 6 4 3
   - (b) ♥ Q J 10 3 2
   - (c) ♥ 8 6 3
   - (d) ♣ K Q 6 3
   - (e) ♠ J 10 8 5 2
   - (f) ♥ Q 10 9 2
   - (g) ♦ 9 7 5 2
   - (h) ♣ J 7 6

2. What card would you lead from the following holdings against a contract of 4♥?

   - (a) ♠ K J 3
   - (b) ♦ 10 6
   - (c) ♣ K Q 6 3
   - (d) ♠ A K 6 2
   - (e) ♦ A 9 7 4
   - (f) ♣ K 10 9 3

3. Partner leads the ♦A against a suit contract. What card would you play from (a) ♦Q-8-2 (b) ♦ 10-7-3. Why?

4.

<pre>
                        ♥ K Q J 10 4
    ♥ 2   ┌─────────────┐   ♥ 8 7 3
                      └─────────────┘
                        ♥ 5
</pre>

   Declarer leads the ♥5 from his hand to partner's ♥2 and dummy's ♥K. Which card do you play and why?

5. You are defending a contract of 4♥ and on the second round of trumps your partner discards the ♦9. What do you think this discard means?

ANSWERS

1. Against a notrump contract you would lead these cards:

   (a) ♠4   The fourth-best card from a suit containing an honor.

   (b) ♥Q   Top of a sequence

   (c) ♥8   Top-of-nothing from three spot cards (but lead the ♥3 if partner has bid the suit and you have not raised).

   (d) ♣3   Fourth-best card when only two honors are held

   (e) ♠J   Top of a broken sequence.

   (f) ♥10   Top of an interior sequence.

   (g) ♦7   Second-best card from four or more spot cards.

   (h) ♣6   Low from three cards headed by an honor.

2. Against a suit contract you would lead these cards:

   (a) ♠3   Bottom of three cards headed by an honor, unless you have two touching honors.

   (b) ♦10   Top of a doubleton.

   (c) ♣K   Against a suit contract only, lead the top honor from two touching honors.

   (d) ♠A   Ace from ace-king.

   (e) ♦A   Not an attractive lead, but against a suit contract never underlead an ace.

   (f) ♣10   Top of an interior sequence.

3. An attitude signal tells your partner whether you would like him to continue the suit he has just led. A high card encourages a continuation and a low card discourages. When partner leads the ♦A and you hold ♦Q-8-2, you should signal with the ♦8 to encourage a continuation. If instead you hold ♦10-7-3 you should play the ♦3 to discourage. The purpose behind such a signal is to indicate your holding in the suit, in order to assist partner's defense.

4. Play the ♥3, to indicate an odd number of cards. A count signal tells partner whether you hold an odd or an even number of cards in the suit led. You give such a signal when declarer leads a suit and you do not have to play high in an attempt to win the trick. The purpose of such a signal is to allow your partner to know how many cards you (and consequently the declarer) hold in the suit.

5. A high discard, such as the ♦9, shows that partner has strength in that suit, here diamonds. It will probably be best for you to lead this suit when you gain the lead. A low discard instead, such as the ♣3, would indicate that partner had no special interest in the suit discarded.

THIRD-HAND PLAY

Strong reasons make strong actions.

William Shakespeare

We know you are looking forward to adding some spectacular defensive coups to your repertoire. We will come to those in due course (that's a promise). Meanwhile, it is our duty to point out that ignorance of such splendors as the Deschapelles Coup will not cost you very much in a lifetime of playing bridge. Many more tricks are squandered on defense by choosing the wrong card to play to a trick. So, in this early chapter we will cast an eye in that direction. We will look at the general rules for playing in the third seat, paying particular attention to situations where it may be right to break the rules.

Very soon after you started playing bridge, someone undoubtedly told you that 'third hand plays high'. Yes, indeed. The reason you play high is to prevent declarer from scoring an undeserved trick with some low card in his hand:

♣ 7 4 2

♣ Q 9 6 3   □   ♣ K 10 8 5

♣ A J

Partner leads the ♣3 and you play the ♣K (third hand high). This forces declarer's ace and partner will now score a trick with the queen. Suppose you are too mean to part with the king and play the ♣10 instead. Declarer will be ecstatic: he will win with the ♣J and score two tricks in the suit. So, when partner leads a low card and dummy has small cards in the suit, it is essential to play high in the third seat.

What if dummy has a high card in the suit led?

Life is not so easy in the third seat when dummy holds a high card in the suit that has been led. Suppose you are East here:

```
            ♥ J 6 4
♥ Q 9 8 2   [        ]   ♥ K 10 3
            ♥ A 7 5
```

West leads the ♥2 against a contract such as 4♠. Since it would be poor play (against a suit contract) to lead the ♥2 rather than the ♥K from ♥K-Q-8-2, declarer knows that there is no point in playing the jack from dummy. He plays low instead and you must find the best play in the East seat. Which card would you choose?

Following the unqualified guideline 'third hand high', some players would play the king. Not the best! Declarer wins with the ace and will subsequently score an undeserved second heart trick with dummy's jack. You must keep the ♥K to deal with dummy's ♥J and should therefore play the ♥10 instead. Declarer wins with the ace and the defense will now score two heart tricks with the king and queen. Such a defensive play is known as 'finessing against the dummy'.

As a general rule:

in third seat, when your top card can beat dummy's honor, insert your second-highest card when it is the nine or higher and dummy plays low.

What if you have two cards of equal rank?

Suppose partner leads a low card and, in the third seat, you have two touching honors (such as the queen and jack). Which one should you play?

```
            ♠ 9 6 4
♠ K 10 7 2  [        ]   ♠ Q J 5
            ♠ A 8 3
```

West leads the ♠2, dummy playing low, and the correct play in the East seat is to *play the lower (or lowest) of touching honors*. Here the ♠J will force South's ♠A. When your partner gains the lead later in the play, he will know that you hold the ♠Q; otherwise declarer would have taken the ♠J with the ♠Q. So West can confidently continue spades.

Suppose the cards lie differently:

```
                    ♠ 9 6 4
  ♠ K 10 7 2       [          ]        ♠ Q 8 5
                    ♠ A J 3
```

West leads the ♠2 to your ♠Q and South's ♠A. Since you would have played the ♠J from ♠Q-J, West *knows* that South holds the ♠J! This time, therefore, he will not continue the suit when he gains the lead. To do so would set up South's ♠J.

You follow the same method even when the touching cards are not the two highest in your suit:

```
                    ♣ Q 6 4
  ♣ J 8 7 2        [          ]        ♣ K 10 9
                    ♣ A 5 3
```

West leads the ♣2 against a suit contract and dummy plays the ♣4. Since it is a sin to underlead an ace against a suit contract, you know that South holds the ♣A. Your correct card is the ♣9, the lower of touching cards. When this forces the ace, your partner will know that he should play another club at his first opportunity.

Suppose that the cards lie like this instead:

```
                    ♣ Q 6 4
  ♣ J 8 7 2        [          ]        ♣ K 10 5
                    ♣ A 9 3
```

Now you play the ♣10 in the third seat, won with the ♣A, and partner can deduce that South holds the ♣9. It will not therefore be safe for West to play this suit again. (Declarer could run the second lead to his ♣9, forcing your ♣K and setting up dummy's ♣Q.)

When should you break the 'third hand high' rule?

It is a somewhat annoying fact of bridge life that most so-called rules of how to play or defend have exceptions to them. There are several exceptions to the rule of 'third hand high' and the time has come to take a look at them.

One exception arises when partner leads a jack against a suit contract and you hold the king — this sort of position:

```
                    ♥ 9 4 3
  ♥ J 10 5         [          ]        ♥ K 8 6 2
                    ♥ A Q 7
```

If West had led the ♥J against a notrump contract, it would be possible that he was leading from ♥A-J-10-4. To prevent declarer from scoring an undeserved trick with his ♥Q-x, you might play the king.

Here, however, the ♥J has been led against a suit contract. Since partner would not make such a lead from ♥A-J-10, you can place declarer with both the ace and queen. You should therefore retain the ♥K, contenting yourself with an encouraging ♥8. If instead you waste your king on the first round, your partner will not be able to continue the suit safely when he next gains the lead.

Many players go wrong in the next situation. Imagine you are sitting East here:

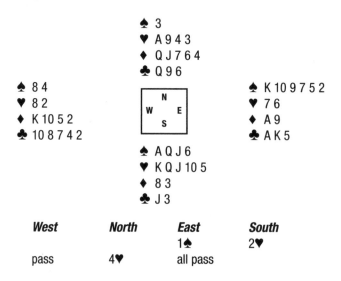

West leads the ♥2 and the ♥7 is played from dummy. Which card should you play?

It cannot possibly be right to play the ♥J! Declarer will win the trick with whatever high card he holds (the king or queen) and subsequently finesse dummy's ♥10. He will score three heart tricks. So play low instead. Declarer wins cheaply with dummy's ♥7, yes, but he will still lose a trick in the suit. (You know that West cannot hold something like ♥K-Q-5-2 because, against a suit contract, he would then have led the king.)

Notice that if you faced the same situation when defending a notrump contract, you might well play the ♥J in the hope that partner did indeed hold ♥K-Q-5-2.

Another common situation where you should break the third-hand-high rule is when you have only one honor and can tell from the lead that partner does not hold any honors himself. Look at this deal:

The defenders have four quick tricks to cash but, naturally enough, West leads the ♠8. How should you defend with the East cards?

Time and again, you will see defenders playing the ♠K, after which the contract will be made. Declarer wins with the ace, draws trumps in two rounds, and throws two of dummy's clubs on the ♠Q-J. Eventually he will be able to ruff a club and a spade in dummy, giving him ten tricks.

It is not at all difficult for East to read the spade situation. Partner's ♠8, a high spot card, clearly denies any honor in the suit. South is therefore marked with the ♠A-Q-J and will score three spade tricks if you play the ♠K on the first trick. Play a low card instead and declarer will make only two spade tricks. He will have no way to avoid four losers in the minor suits and will go down.

Summary

✓ When partner leads a spot card and dummy has no honor in the suit, it is usually right to play high in the third seat. Your objective is to prevent declarer from scoring an undeserved trick. Even if your card is beaten, you may have promoted one or more cards in your partner's hand.

✓ When partner has led a high spot card, denying an honor, and you hold only one honor in the suit (not the ace), it will often be wrong to play this card.

✓ When you are playing from cards of equal value, in the third seat, you should play the lower (or lowest) card. For example, you must play the queen from K-Q-6-3. This will help your partner read the lie of the suit. If you play the king instead, you will be telling partner you do not have the queen.

✓ When partner leads a low card and dummy has an honor in the suit, it is often right for you to retain a higher honor and play your second-highest card. For example, if partner leads the ♣4 and dummy has ♣Q-7-3, you should play the 10 from ♣K-10-2 if dummy does not play the queen.

THIRD-HAND PLAY

NOW TRY THESE...

1. Partner leads the ♠Q. How will you defend?

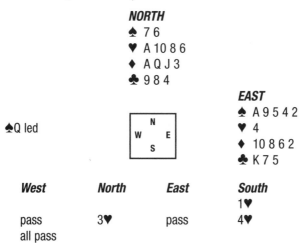

NORTH
- ♠ 7 6
- ♥ A 10 8 6
- ♦ A Q J 3
- ♣ 9 8 4

EAST
- ♠ A 9 5 4 2
- ♥ 4
- ♦ 10 8 6 2
- ♣ K 7 5

♠Q led

West	North	East	South
			1♥
pass	3♥	pass	4♥
all pass			

2. Your partner leads the ♥2 against South's small slam in spades. Declarer plays low from dummy. What is your plan for the defense?

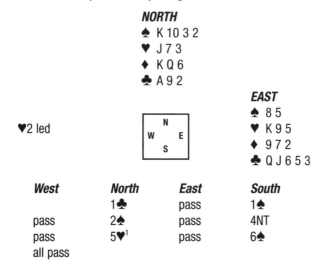

NORTH
- ♠ K 10 3 2
- ♥ J 7 3
- ♦ K Q 6
- ♣ A 9 2

EAST
- ♠ 8 5
- ♥ K 9 5
- ♦ 9 7 2
- ♣ Q J 6 5 3

♥2 led

West	North	East	South
	1♣	pass	1♠
pass	2♠	pass	4NT
pass	5♥[1]	pass	6♠
all pass			

1. Showing two keycards without the trump queen. Playing regular Blackwood, North would respond 5♦, showing one ace.

ANSWERS

1.

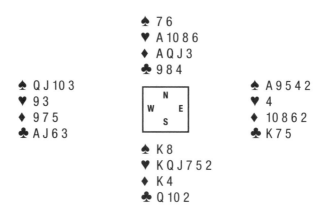

Your partner leads the ♠Q against South's game in hearts. You should play 'third hand high' and win with the ♠A. If you mistakenly play low instead, declarer might score a trick with a singleton ♠K. When the cards lie as in the diagram, South will follow with the ♠8. You now need three club tricks to beat the contract, so switch to that suit.

2.

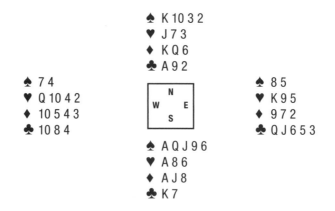

Your partner leads the ♥2 against South's small slam in spades. If you play the ♥K, declarer will win with the ♥A, draw trumps and set up the ♥J for his twelfth trick. You must therefore hope that partner has led from the Q-10. Play the ♥9 and you will force South's ♥A, beating the slam.

CHAPTER

OPENING LEADS AGAINST A NOTRUMP CONTRACT

> The best way to have a good idea is to have lots of good ideas.
>
> **Linus Pauling**

Most notrump contracts turn out to be a race between declarer and the defenders. Each side is trying to set up their strongest suit (or suits), hoping to be first to score the tricks that they need. Suppose you are defending 3NT. You need five tricks to beat the contract and, unless you have reason to place partner with a strong suit somewhere, you will normally lead your own longest and strongest suit. As we saw in Chapter 1, you lead the fourth-best card in the suit unless you hold some sort of sequence there.

Suppose the opponents have bid 1NT-3NT and you are lucky enough to hold something like ♠K-Q-J-8-3. This is a splendid suit to lead for two reasons. Firstly, there is every chance of setting up four tricks for the defense. Secondly, a lead of the ♠K is unlikely to give declarer an extra trick in the suit.

Now give yourself a different hand, one that includes ♥K-J-7-5-2. Again this is a fine suit to lead against 3NT. You still have a good chance of setting up several defensive tricks. If partner can produce the ace or queen of the suit, you might not give away a trick in the process. This time, however, you have no honor sequence so you lead the ♥5, fourth best.

Next let's look at some four-card holdings. A suit such as ♦K-Q-J-5 gives you an excellent lead. The lesser holdings of ♦K-J-8-2 and ♦K-10-8-2 are quite respectable too. When you make the intermediate cards worse, leaving you with a suit such as ♦K-7-6-2 or ♦Q-8-5-3, the situation is much less promising. You could lose on two fronts. First, you are more likely to give away a trick by leading from a suit with no good second-best card. Second, the prospect of establishing some winners is not so bright. That said, you may be forced to lead such a suit when nothing better is available.

You get the idea, then. When considering a particular opening lead against a notrump contract, you must weigh up both the prospect of setting up tricks for the defenders and the potential risk of giving declarer an extra trick. When there is a worthwhile chance of establishing several winners for the defense, you are happy to risk giving away a trick. You should be less willing to lead from four cards to an honor when your intermediate cards are poor. In such a situation, you may well prefer to make a 'passive lead'. In other words you will lead from a suit such as 9-8-6-2 or 10-9-5, where there will be less chance of giving away a trick. Sometimes partner will be strong in the suit that you lead and it will work out well constructively too.

Let's look at a full hand of thirteen cards. Suppose the bidding has been: 1NT-3NT and you have to find a lead from:

♠ J 7 6 2 ♥ 10 9 3 ♦ A 8 6 ♣ Q 7 4

A spade lead is not promising. Leading from a jack is often one of the most expensive leads you can make (more dangerous than leading from a king or a queen). Even if you find your partner with a spade honor — the ace, king or queen — you are more likely than not to give declarer an extra trick in the suit. So lead the ♥10 instead.

Which four-card suit should I lead?

Suppose the opponents have bid 1NT-3NT and you have to find a lead from this hand:

♠ K 7 6 2 ♥ Q 10 8 3 ♦ J 8 4 ♣ 8 5

You would lead the ♥3 because the presence of the ten and eight makes it less likely that the lead will give declarer an extra trick.

You can understand a fair amount about notrump leads simply by comparing the two combinations A-Q-x-x-x and A-Q-x-x. This five-card holding is regarded as one of the best opening leads available at notrump. There is a big risk of giving away a trick, yes, but also a great prospect of setting up four defensive tricks. However, you sometimes hear this four-card holding described as 'one of the worst leads in the game' (a slight exaggeration!). That's because you are just as likely to give away a trick and will have less compensation in terms of the number of tricks you can create.

Now suppose that you have two four-card suits that are similar in nature:

♠ A 4　♥ K 10 7 2　♦ Q 10 6 4　♣ 9 8 3

It may appear to be a complete guess which red suit to lead. In such a situation you should prefer to lead a major suit rather than a minor suit. Can you see why? It's because responder might have used Stayman if he held four hearts. He is therefore more likely to hold four diamonds than four hearts.

What if the opponents have bid your suits?

Most of the time, it will not be a good idea to lead a suit that has been bid naturally by the opponents. Suppose you have to find a lead here, as West:

♠ K 9 6 3　♥ Q 10 9 6　♦ 4 2　♣ 8 7 3

West	North	East	South
			1♥
pass	1♠	pass	1NT
pass	3NT	all pass	

There is little point in leading either of the major suits after this auction. A club is better than a diamond because you hold three cards there. This means you will be able to continue playing the suit should you gain the lead in the majors. Lead the ♣8 (top of nothing).

What should you lead when you are very weak?

When you have the chance of an entry or two in your hand, it makes good sense to lead from your own strongest suit. When instead you are very weak and expect partner to have the entries, it may be better to try to find partner's long suit. Suppose the opponents bid 1NT-3NT and you must find a lead from this hand:

♠ J 10 3　♥ 7 6　♦ 9 8 6 5 2　♣ 10 8 2

Hoping to set up the diamonds and enjoy the long cards in the suit is a distant prospect. For a start, if partner held four diamonds, the opponents would almost certainly have been playing in a major suit rather than notrump. So, don't look for miracles with a diamond lead; try the ♠J instead. This is better than leading a club for two reasons. First, you have a potentially useful honor holding in spades, which may help to force out declarer's stoppers in the suit. Second, with other things being equal, it is better to lead a major suit than a minor suit. That's because the responder might have employed Stayman if he held a four-card major.

What if partner has bid a suit?

When partner has bid a suit, particularly when he has overcalled, you should normally lead that suit. Suppose you are on lead against 3NT with this hand:

♠ Q 10 8 6 3　♥ 7 6　♦ K 6 3　♣ 9 7 4

If the bidding has been 1NT-3NT, you will naturally lead the ♠6. Suppose instead that your partner has overcalled 1♥ over your left-hand opponent's opening bid of one of a minor. Now you should lead the ♥7. Indeed, partner may have bid his hearts mainly with the intention of suggesting a heart lead to you.

Leading against 6NT

Suppose that you have a suit such as ♠K-J-8-6-2. This represents a fine opening lead against 3NT, of course. You are willing to risk giving away a trick initially, because there is a compensating chance that you might be able to set up the suit and score several tricks from it.

The notion of 'eventually setting up the suit' does not apply against 6NT, when the defenders will gain the lead at most once more (unless the contract is already down anyway). As a general rule, you should *make a passive lead against 6NT*. Indeed, you should base your whole opening lead strategy on trying to avoid giving away a trick. Anyone who leads from a holding such as ♠K-J-8-6-2 against 6NT is telling the world that he is an inexperienced player. Pick a different, safer, suit to lead.

Look at this typical 6NT deal:

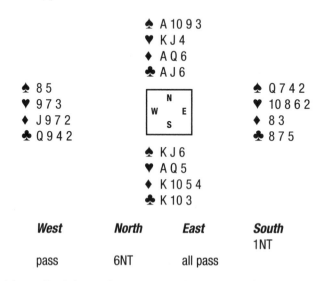

	♠ A 10 9 3	
	♥ K J 4	
	♦ A Q 6	
	♣ A J 6	

West	North	East	South
			1NT
pass	6NT	all pass	

What would you lead from the West hand? It is incredibly dangerous to lead a diamond or a club! There is every chance that leading from an honor will give away a trick or save declarer a guess in the suit — in fact that is exactly what would happen on this deal. Which is safer, do you think, to lead from a ♠8-5 or ♥9-7-3? It is slightly safer to lead from the tripleton. When you have a double-ton, there is a greater chance that your partner holds four cards to the queen or jack. By leading the suit, you might give away the position.

So, on this deal, you should lead the ♥9 (top of nothing). Declarer may still make the contract, or he may not. At least you will not have handed it to him on a plate.

Of course, one particular layout proves nothing at all. Sometimes declarer will hold ♥A-J-x opposite K-10-x and a heart lead will save him a guess in the suit. You just have to play with the odds and choose the lead that looks safest. In the long run it will cost you a bundle to lead from an honor against 6NT contracts.

Summary

✓ When choosing a lead against a notrump contract, you must compare two factors, the chance of setting up tricks in the suit and the risk of giving away a trick.

✓ Leading from a sequence (such as Q-J-10-5) is good for two reasons. You have an excellent chance of establishing tricks for the defense and there is relatively little risk of giving declarer an extra trick.

✓ Leading from a strong four-card suit such as K-J-7-2 or Q-J-8-5 is a fair prospect. When your second-best card is lower, such as K-7-6-2 or Q-8-6-2, this is a much less attractive lead. You may prefer a safer lead from a different suit.

✓ It is usually wrong to lead your own strongest suit when it has been bid by the opponents.

✓ When your own hand is very weak, it may be a waste of time to lead your longest suit. Even if you can establish it, you will not be able to gain the lead to cash the long cards. In such a situation it might be best to lead a short suit (prefer x-x-x to x-x) in the hope that partner will have a strong holding there.

✓ Choose a passive lead against 6NT. It is rarely right to lead away from an honor.

OPENING LEADS AGAINST A NOTRUMP CONTRACT

NOW TRY THESE...

1. What would you lead from each of the West hands shown below?

(a)	♠ K 10 3 2	(b)	♠ 10 9 8 5	(c)	♠ 10 5
	♥ 10 8 3		♥ 7		♥ J 10 4
	♦ K 10 6 4		♦ K Q 10 8 3		♦ 10 8 7 2
	♣ 9 4		♣ A 9 2		♣ 9 7 6 2

West	North	East	South
			1NT
pass	3NT	all pass	

2. What would you lead from each of the West hands shown below?

(a)	♠ J 7 3	(b)	♠ 8 6 4	(c)	♠ Q 10 5 3
	♥ 10 8		♥ 10 9 8 2		♥ 7 6 3
	♦ K J 6 4 2		♦ Q J 5		♦ Q 2
	♣ J 10 4		♣ 8 5 3		♣ K 10 7 4

West	North	East	South
			1♦
pass	1♥	pass	1NT
pass	3NT	all pass	

3. What would you lead from each of the West hands shown below?

(a)	♠ 7 5 4	(b)	♠ Q 8 2	(c)	♠ 9 4
	♥ Q 7 6		♥ Q 6		♥ K J 6 2
	♦ Q 10 9 7 3		♦ Q 9 8 5		♦ J 8 3
	♣ 6 3		♣ J 7 3 2		♣ 9 7 6 2

West	North	East	South
			1NT
pass	6NT	all pass	

ANSWERS

1   (a) ♠2   Prefer a major suit to a minor suit.

    (b) ♦K   Lead the top of a broken sequence. You are more likely to score the five tricks you need after a diamond lead than a spade lead.

    (c) ♥J   A minor-suit lead, when your hand is so weak, would rarely be productive. A tripleton lead is a better prospect than a doubleton lead, particular when the tripleton contains two honors.

2   (a) ♣J   It would be a poor idea to lead a diamond because South has bid the suit. The ♣J is more constructive than a low spade because you have two honors in the suit.

    (b) ♣8   You hold only 3 points yourself and must hope that partner holds a fair hand in order to beat the contract. Since he could have overcalled at the one-level if he held five spades, it is more likely that you will find him with a good club suit.

    (c) ♠3   One opponent or the other might have looked for a spade fit if they held four cards in the suit. It is therefore more promising to lead a spade than a club.

3   (a) ♠7   To lead from either of your queens would be a serious mistake — very likely indeed to give a trick away. A tripleton lead is more likely to be safe than a doubleton lead.

    (b) ♣2   You don't want to lead away from an honor but you will have to! The least of evils is a low club. That's because you have four cards in the suit and declarer may have correspondingly short holdings, something like ♣A-Q-x opposite ♣K-x-x. A diamond lead might give declarer an undeserved trick with the ♦J. A lead of either major suit would be incredibly risky.

    (c) ♣7   A club lead is safest. (Most players do not lead top-of-nothing from a four-card suit, preferring to lead the ♣7. That's because your ♣9 will sometimes be valuable to guard the fourth round of clubs.)

CHAPTER

SECOND-HAND PLAY

We can try to avoid making choices by doing nothing, but even that is a decision.

Gary Collins

You will recall that back in Chapter 2 we discussed basic play in the third seat. The general rule was 'third hand plays high' but, as always, there were some exceptions. The time has come to look at the main concepts of defending in the second seat, when declarer has led to a trick from one hand or another. The basic rule in this case, as you doubtless know, is 'second hand plays low'. In this chapter we will see why it is usually a good idea. In later chapters on maintaining defensive communications and breaking declarer's communications we will see some exceptions to this general guideline.

Play low to avoid giving declarer an extra trick

When you hold an ace on defense, you hope to capture a high card with it. If instead you gather two lowly spot cards, all declarer's honors will move up one notch. Imagine that declarer is playing in a major-suit contract and has this side suit:

♣ A 8 6   ♣ K 10 7 4   ♣ J 9 5 3

♣ Q 2

What should you do when declarer leads the ♣2? Second hand plays low! If you rise with the ♣A, you will find three very small fish in your net: the ♣4, ♣3 and ♣2. Subsequently, declarer will score tricks with both the queen and king of the suit. Play low on the first round instead and declarer cannot score more than one trick. Whether or not he chooses to finesse the ♣10, you will catch a big fish in your net on the next round: South's ♣Q.

Perhaps you are worried that declarer holds a singleton club and you will never score your ace if you play low. It's possible. Even in that case, rising with the ♣A might not help you very much; declarer will usually be able to throw a loser on the established ♣K. In general, you should rise with the ace only if doing so will ensure beating the contract.

Sometimes it is not easy to tell whether to play low or high. Suppose declarer has this side suit:

      ♣ Q 4

♣ K 10 5 3   ♣ A 9 8 6

      ♣ J 7 2

Declarer leads the ♣2 from his hand. Should you play the ♣K or not? Rise with the king here, catching three small cards, and you will give declarer an undeserved trick. On the other hand, the suit might lie like this instead:

      ♣ Q 4

♣ K 10 5 3   ♣ J 9 8 6

      ♣ A 7 2

This time it might be better to rise with the ♣K, ensuring that you score a trick in the suit. Well, we never said that defending was easy. Sometimes you have to guess how the cards lie. On many deals you would be able to tell from the bidding, or the play in other suits, whether declarer was likely to hold the ♣A.

Play low to put declarer to a guess

Playing low in the second seat may give declarer a tricky guess. Rise with a high honor instead and you save him that guess. Suppose declarer is playing in a small slam and must lose only one trick from this side suit:

      ♥ K J 5

♥ A 10 7 3   ♥ Q 9 6 2

      ♥ 8 4

He leads the ♥4 from his hand, hoping to guess correctly which honor to play from dummy. If you rise with the ace (or even hesitate while you decide whether to play the ace), you will give declarer the slam! Play low instead, giving nothing away, and declarer may well try the jack from dummy.

Here is a full deal on the same theme:

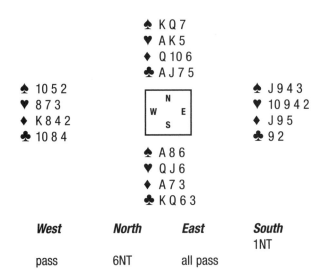

West	North	East	South
			1NT
pass	6NT	all pass	

Sitting West, you make the safe lead of the ♥8 against 6NT. Declarer wins with dummy's ♥A, crosses to his hand with the ♣K and leads the ♦3. How will you defend?

Declarer can see eleven top tricks and therefore needs to score a second diamond trick. This will require a successful guess when the outstanding diamond honors are split. If you rise with the ♦K, you will save declarer this guess; he will score two diamond tricks with the ace and queen, making the contract. If you spend even a moment or two considering the play of the king, you will give away the diamond position and the slam with it.

Whether or not you have had time to take a look at the other suits, you should play a smooth low card when a diamond is led. What you do know is that East *must* hold the ♦J. If declarer's diamonds were headed by the ace-jack, he would have led the suit from dummy, finessing against the king. Play low immediately and there is every chance that declarer will guess wrongly in the suit and go down.

Should you split your honors?

When you have touching honors in the second seat (K-Q-5-2, for example, or Q-J-8), you may have to judge whether to play one of them on the first round. If you do, this is known as 'splitting your honors'. Look at this situation:

```
                          ♦ A 10 4
                          ┌─────────┐
          ♦ Q J 5         └─────────┘         ♦ 8 7 3
                          ♦ K 9 6 2
```

Declarer leads the ♦2 from his hand. If you play 'low in second seat', contributing the ♦5, declarer will play dummy's ♦10. To his surprise and delight, he will then score four diamond tricks! You must split your honors (most players prefer to play the higher honor, the queen here). Declarer will win with dummy's ♦A and you will later score a trick in the suit.

   It was easy to make the right play in the previous position, because you could see the A-10-4 sitting over you. Suppose North had been declarer and he had led the ♦2 from dummy (South). Since the king was visible in dummy and you could be pretty sure that declarer held the ace, you would again split your honors. Even if East did happen to hold the ♦A, it would still be right for you to play an honor.

   When declarer leads towards his hand and there is no high honor in dummy, it can be a mistake to split your honors. Suppose declarer reaches game in spades and this is his trump suit:

```
                          ♠ 7 4 2
                          ┌─────────┐
          ♠ 10            └─────────┘         ♠ Q J 6
                          ♠ A K 9 8 5 3
```

The ♠2 is led from dummy and you are sitting East. If you play one of your honors, declarer will win and the ♠10 will fall from West. Declarer can then re-enter dummy, finesse against your remaining honor and lose no trick in the suit. Instead you should play low on the first round. Declarer will then lose a trick in the suit.

   If declarer holds ♠A-K-10-8-3 and intends to finesse on the first round, there is nothing you can do about it anyway. If instead he holds ♠A-K-10-x-x-x, he probably has no intention of finessing. Don't make him change his mind by splitting your honors!

What if a singleton is led from dummy?

There is one situation that you will meet time and time again. Playing in a suit contract, declarer leads a side-suit singleton from dummy. You hold the ace in the second seat. Should you play the ace or not? You may be surprised to hear that it is normally best to play low. Look at this deal:

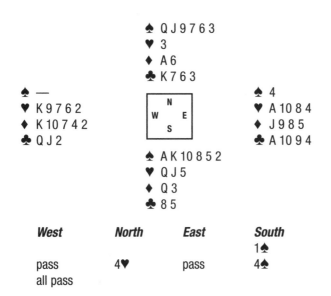

♠ Q J 9 7 6 3
♥ 3
♦ A 6
♣ K 7 6 3

♠ —
♥ K 9 7 6 2
♦ K 10 7 4 2
♣ Q J 2

♠ 4
♥ A 10 8 4
♦ J 9 8 5
♣ A 10 9 4

♠ A K 10 8 5 2
♥ Q J 5
♦ Q 3
♣ 8 5

West	North	East	South
			1♠
pass	4♥	pass	4♠
all pass			

North's 4♥ is a splinter bid, showing a sound raise to game with at most one heart. Your partner, West, leads the ♣Q against 4♠. Realizing that you must hold the ace, declarer plays low in dummy and the queen wins. West's ♣J takes the next trick and he continues with a club to your ten, ruffed by South. Declarer plays a trump to the queen and leads dummy's singleton heart. How should you defend?

If you rise with the ♥A, catching nothing of value in your fishing net, there are two main ways that this might prove expensive. When the cards lie as in the diagram, declarer will be able to take a ruffing finesse on the next round, leading his ♥Q-J through your partner's ♥K. He will then be able to discard dummy's diamond loser on the established winner in hearts.

Another possibility is that South holds ♥K-J-x. If you rise with the ♥A you will save him a guess. Play low smoothly and he is likely to place the ♥A with your partner (that's because most defenders rise with the ace when they hold it), Declarer will finesse the ♥J and not score a trick from the suit. He will lose one trick in each red suit as well as two clubs, going down one.

As a general rule, you should rise with an ace only when you think that this may beat the contract.

Summary

✓ As a general rule, you should play low in second seat. This is because you hope to capture an honor with a big card such as an ace or king.

✓ Another good reason to play low in the second seat is that you may leave declarer with a guess. Suppose declarer leads towards a K-J holding and you hold the ace in second position. If you rise with the ace, you will save him a guess.

✓ Split your honors in second seat when you fear that declarer will otherwise finesse and you will not score either of your high cards.

✓ It is often wrong to rise with the ace when declarer leads a side-suit singleton from dummy. If he holds K-J-x-x, you will save him a guess. If instead he holds Q-J-x-x, you will set up a ruffing finesse against partner's king. In general, rise with the ace only when you can see a chance of beating the contract by doing so.

SECOND-HAND PLAY

NOW TRY THESE...

1. Your partner leads the ♠10 against South's 6NT. Declarer wins with dummy's ace and surprises you by leading the ♥2. How will you defend?

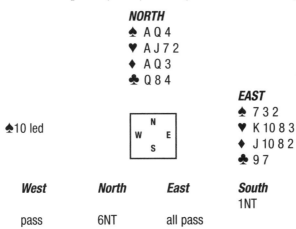

NORTH
♠ A Q 4
♥ A J 7 2
♦ A Q 3
♣ Q 8 4

EAST
♠ 7 3 2
♥ K 10 8 3
♦ J 10 8 2
♣ 9 7

♠10 led

West	North	East	South
			1NT
pass	6NT	all pass	

2. You lead the ♦10. Declarer wins with the ♦A and leads the ♠3 towards dummy. Will you split your spade honors or not? What is the reason for your decision?

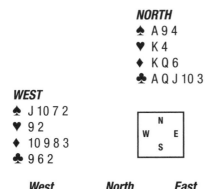

NORTH
♠ A 9 4
♥ K 4
♦ K Q 6
♣ A Q J 10 3

WEST
♠ J 10 7 2
♥ 9 2
♦ 10 9 8 3
♣ 9 6 2

West	North	East	South
	1♣	pass	1♠
pass	2NT	pass	3♥
pass	3♠	pass	4NT
pass	5♥	pass	6♠
all pass			

ANSWERS

1.

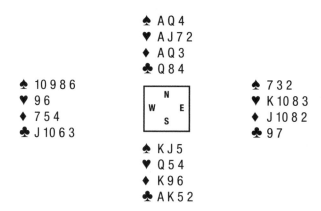

Your partner leads the ♠10 against South's 6NT. Declarer wins with dummy's ace and surprises you somewhat by leading the ♥2. How will you defend? Declarer surely holds the ♥Q. If you rise with the ♥K (collecting three embarrassingly small fish in your net) declarer will make three heart tricks. The slam will be his. Play 'second hand low' and declarer will score only two heart tricks, going down one.

2.

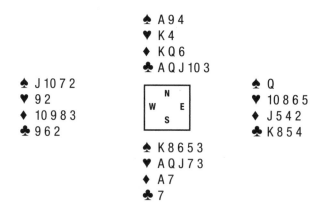

You lead the ♦10 against 6♠. Declarer wins with the ♦A and leads the ♠3 towards dummy. You should not split your spade honors. Whatever trump holding declarer has, there is no reason whatsoever to expect him to finesse the ♠9 if you play the ♠2. Play 'second hand low' and you score two trump tricks. Split your honors and declarer will make the slam.

CHAPTER

OPENING LEADS AGAINST A SUIT CONTRACT

 Take calculated risks. That is quite different from being rash.

George S. Patton

The fate of many a contract hangs on the opening lead. Is it easy to choose the best opening lead against a suit contract? No! That's because there are so many types of opening lead that can prove successful. A short-suit lead may allow you to score a ruff. An attacking lead from an honor in a side suit may let you score (or establish) some winners before declarer has a chance to discard his losers. A trump lead may prevent declarer from taking some ruffs. Finally, a passive lead — from a suit such as 8-7-3 — may beat the contract merely because it does not give a trick away. How can you possibly choose the winning lead consistently when there are so many options?

Choosing the opening lead is always a gamble, to some extent, but you can bend the odds in your favor by choosing leads that have a better chance of succeeding that any of the alternatives.

In the opening chapter of this book we noted which card you should lead from various holdings in a suit. That much is easy to learn. Deciding which of the four suits to lead is sometimes a difficult decision. In this chapter we will look in turn at the various types of lead against a suit contract. Which are good bets, worthy of our patronage, and which are poor risks?

When should you lead a short suit?

A singleton is often a good opening lead, particularly against a high-level contract. You will score a ruff when partner holds the ace of the suit led; you may also score a ruff when partner has a quick entry in trumps.

There are a few circumstances in which a singleton lead becomes less attractive. The most important one is when the opponents have bid that suit. You are less likely to find partner with the ace in this case. Also, you may be leading through partner's honor (or honors) in the suit, making it easier for declarer to assemble his tricks.

It is not very attractive to lead a singleton honor either. Suppose declarer is in 4♠ and you hold a singleton ♦J. Such an opening lead might work well occasionally, but you could also find the suit divided like this:

Your lead of the ♦J is covered by the queen, king and ace. A subsequent finesse of the ♦8 succeeds and declarer scores three tricks from the suit. Left to his own devices, declarer will probably lose at least one diamond trick and possibly two.

A singleton is a particularly potent opening lead against a small slam. However, you are hoping that partner will hold a useful ace (in the suit led or in trumps). This is not at all likely when you hold an ace in your own hand. In such a situation you should look elsewhere for your lead.

How about leading a doubleton? In our opinion, such leads are overrated and generally a poor idea. You are less likely to receive a ruff because declarer may be able to win the first or second round of the suit and draw trumps.

Particularly expensive are leads from a doubleton honor. When you lead from K-x, it is possible that you will find partner with the ace and score a ruff on the third round. Every now and again, yes, but you will give away a lot of tricks in the meantime. Even more expensive and less likely to be productive are leads from Q-x or J-x. Use them only as a last resort, except (of course) when partner has bid the suit.

A short-suit lead has more chance of succeeding when you hold a trump entry such as the ace or king. Even if partner cannot win and give you a ruff immediately, you may well have a second chance when you win with your trump honor. However, you should usually not lead a short suit if your potential ruff would be with a natural trump trick, from a trump holding like Q-J-10 for example.

When should you make an attacking lead?

In the long run, one of the best leads to make is to attack from strength in an unbid side suit. Suppose you have to find a lead from these West cards:

West
♠ Q 9 3 ♥ K J 8 2 ♦ J 9 6 ♣ 10 8 5

West	North	East	South
			1♠
pass	2♣	pass	2♠
pass	4♠	all pass	

You can picture the dummy with a fair side suit in clubs. Declarer may well establish this suit to obtain some discards. You must attack in one of the red suits to score (or establish) some winners there before declarer can discard his losers. Which red suit should you lead? A heart is much more promising than a diamond. Why is that? Because if you find your partner with the ♥A or the ♥Q, you will be well on your way to scoring some tricks. If you lead a diamond and find partner with the ♦A or ♦Q, the most likely effect is that you will have given away a trick!

This is the sort of layout that you are hoping for:

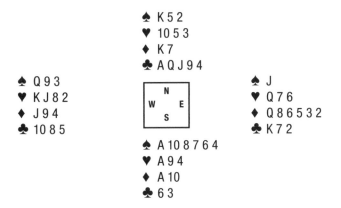

You lead the ♥2 against South's spade game and partner produces the ♥Q. Your attacking lead has set up two heart tricks and declarer has no chance to make the contract. After any other opening lead, declarer would have established dummy's club suit and made an overtrick.

"They've chosen a deal where the heart lead happens to work," you may be saying to yourself. It's true but, believe us, with this hand a heart lead is more likely to succeed than any other. You need to score four tricks from somewhere! Unless you set about this objective as quickly as possible, declarer will soon score ten tricks, at least, from his own suits.

What sort of holding should you look for when you decide to make an attacking lead in an unbid side suit? We have already seen that K-J-x-x is promising because either the ace or queen opposite will give you good prospects, but K-10-x-x is fairly good too, with K-9-x-x slightly less attractive. Similarly Q-J-x-x and Q-10-x-x represent better bets than something like Q-8-x-x. In other words, intermediate cards can prove valuable — to assist you in setting up tricks, and also to reduce the risk of giving away a trick.

An opening lead of the ace from Axxx or Axx is rarely right, but there is an exception:

♠ 873 ♥ A852 ♦ K1063 ♣ 94

West	North	East	South
			1♣
pass	1♠	pass	3♣
pass	3♦	pass	4♣
pass	5♣	all pass	

Here North-South avoided 3NT and went for the eleven-trick game. Clearly they are worried about hearts, and you should lead the ♥A.

You will hear inexperienced players saying, "I never lead away from a king." Nod politely, if you like, but such players will never go very far in the game. When an attacking lead is called for, you must be brave! Don't be worried about leading from holdings like K-J-x-x. Indeed, you should look forward to such moments. You want to beat the contract, desperately, and such a lead will give you a great chance of doing so.

When should you lead a trump?

What sort of player tends to say, "When in doubt, lead a trump"? The answer, you will not be surprised to hear, is someone who is usually in doubt as to what to lead! You should lead a trump when the auction positively suggests a trump lead, not because you have no idea what to lead.

Here are some situations where a trump lead may work well:

(a) The responder has given preference to the opener's second suit. After an auction such as 1♠-1NT; 2♦-pass, it is quite possible that the responder has one spade and three diamonds. By leading a trump, you may reduce the number of spade ruffs that can be taken.

(b) Your partner has passed your takeout double, converting it to a penalty double. For example, you double an opening 1♦ bid for takeout and this is passed out. Your partner will have a long, semi-solid trump holding and you should lead a trump to begin the process of drawing declarer's trumps.

(c) You and your partner have the great majority of the points and the opponents have sacrificed against some high-level contract. They are obviously relying on ruffing values to score their tricks. You may be able to reduce these by leading a trump.

(d) On other occasions you may decide to lead a trump because your holdings in the side suits are unattractive. Look at this West hand:

♠ 9 7 3 ♥ K 7 6 2 ♦ J 8 4 ♣ A 10 4

West	North	East	South
			1♠
pass	4♠	all pass	

You rule out a club lead immediately. Unless you also hold the king, it is a very expensive practice to lead from ace-high suits. Nor is it attractive to lead from a jack — that is very likely to give away a trick. If your hearts were K-J-6-2, you would lead a heart, hoping to establish some tricks there. Here your second-best card is a humble seven-spot, so the lead is uninviting. Reluctantly, you make the passive lead of a low trump.

Leading against a slam in a suit

In the chapter on opening leads against notrump contracts we noted that you should generally choose a passive lead against 6NT. The opposite is the case when opponents reach a slam in a suit contract. Given time, they will usually be able to set up twelve tricks in one way or another. Do not give them that time! Make an attacking lead, aiming to set up a second trick to defeat the slam.

♠ 9 8 6 3   ♥ K 3   ♦ 10 9 3   ♣ K 10 7 3

West	North	East	South
			1♥
pass	2♦	pass	3♥
pass	4NT	pass	5♠
pass	6♥	all pass	

What should you lead? You expect to win a trick with the ♥K sitting over the heart bidder. Where can you find a second trick? The best chance is to lead the ♣3. If partner holds the ♣Q, you will set up your ♣K. You may then be able to cash it when you get on lead with the ♥K.

How about leading a spade? It *might* be the winning lead, if dummy held the ♠A and partner had the ♠K sitting over it. All in all, this is less likely than finding partner with the ♣Q.

Summary

✓ A singleton is usually a promising lead, particularly if it is a spot card in an unbid suit. Leading a doubleton is less likely to result in a ruff for the defense. Be particularly reluctant to lead a doubleton honor.

✓ When you suspect a healthy side suit in the dummy, make an attacking lead in an unbid suit.

✓ A sequence such as K-Q-J-x is the most promising attacking lead. Next best is a holding containing two honors (K-Q-x-x or K-J-x-x). A holding such as Q-10-x-x represents a better lead than Q-9-x-x or Q-8-x-x.

✓ It is rarely a good idea to lead from A-x-x-x or A-x-x. (An exception is when the opponents appear to have this suit unguarded and have bypassed 3NT to play in five of a minor.) If you do decide to lead from such a suit, lead the ace rather than a low card.

✓ In general, lead a trump because the bidding tells you that such a lead may be beneficial. Do not fall back on a trump lead because you are nervous of making an attacking lead, even though the auction has suggested that one may be necessary.

✓ Usually make an attacking lead against a small slam in a suit. You must try to set up a second trick for the defense before declarer can establish any discards. (Against 6NT, as we saw in Chapter 3, the opposite is the case. You should generally look for a passive lead.)

OPENING LEADS AGAINST A SUIT CONTRACT

NOW TRY THESE...

1. What would you lead from each of the West hands shown below?

	(a)	(b)	(c)
♠	3 2	9 7 5	10 5
♥	Q 9 7 2	A 10 7 3	K J 3
♦	K 10 8 3	A J 8 4	J 8 7 2
♣	J 9 4	9 2	Q 7 6 2

West	North	East	South
			1♠
pass	2♣	pass	2♠
pass	4♠	all pass	

2. What would you lead from each of the West hands shown below?

	(a)	(b)	(c)
♠	Q J 8 2	J 8 2	Q 8 5 4
♥	Q 9 3	J 6	9 7 6
♦	10 7 4 2	J 9 8 5 2	K J 7 5 2
♣	J 3	J 7 3	6

West	North	East	South
			1♥
pass	3♥	pass	4♥
all pass			

3. What would you lead from each of the West hands shown below?

	(a)	(b)	(c)
♠	7 5	10 2	A 6 4
♥	10 7 6 2	Q J 7	5
♦	K 10 7 3	K 9 6 5 2	10 9 7 4 2
♣	9 6 3	J 6 4	J 7 5 3

West	North	East	South
			1♠
pass	3♣	pass	3♠
pass	4NT	pass	5♦
pass	6♠	all pass	

ANSWERS

1. (a) ♦3 An attacking lead is required and the presence of the ♦10 makes a diamond lead more attractive than a heart lead.

   (b) ♠5 You would like to make an attacking lead, but leading from an ace-high suit is rarely a good idea against a trump contract (unless you also hold the king). So, reluctantly, you fall back on a trump lead.

   (c) ♥3 There is no reason whatsoever to fear making a heart lead. You need four tricks to beat the spade game and some of these will surely have to come from the heart suit.

2. (a) ♠Q It would be horribly dangerous to lead from ♣J-x. The spade lead is easily best because you hold two honors and a good intermediate, the ♠8. Find partner with the ♠A, ♠K or ♠10 and the lead may work well. Lead the queen rather than a low card, to make sure declarer doesn't make a cheap trick with the ♠10.

   (b) ♦5 Everyone hates leading from a jack. When you are forced to do so, choose your longest suit. You are less likely to give away a trick because someone or other will be ruffing the third round.

   (c) ♣6 You have a spot card singleton in an unbid suit, so this is an attractive lead. Since you hold three trumps, you will be able to ruff a club even if partner can't get in until the second round of trumps.

3. (a) ♦3 Make an attacking lead against a suit slam. You hope to make one diamond trick (if partner holds the ♦Q) plus another winner in partner's hand. Once in a while, partner will hold the ♦A, allowing you to score two diamond tricks.

   (b) ♥Q A heart lead is better than a diamond because you hold two honors rather than one. Also, even if a diamond lead would set up a trick in that suit, there is a greater chance that declarer or the dummy will be able to ruff the second round.

   (c) ♦10 Since you hold an ace and the opponents have used Blackwood, you cannot expect partner to hold an ace. So, a singleton lead (which might give away the location of an honor in partner's hand) is unlikely to be productive. Lead the other unbid suit instead.

ACTIVE DEFENSE
OR PASSIVE DEFENSE?

 When it is not necessary to make a decision, it is necessary not to make a decision.

Lord Falkland

What is the most common mistake that inexperienced players make when defending? There can be little doubt about it. They tend to switch from suit to suit, looking for tricks wherever they can. It is rather like fishing for shrimp. If they scoop their net into one pool and don't catch any shrimp, they turn round and scoop their net in a different pool.

Why is this an expensive tactic to follow? Because every time you make the first play in a new suit, you are likely to give a trick away. It has been calculated that leading a new suit costs around half a trick on average. This is a fair enough premium to pay when you lead from ♦K-J-8-5-2 against a notrump contract, because it is reasonable to hope to set up some long cards there eventually. When you are defending a suit contract, you have to be more wary of attacking new suits and giving away tricks unnecessarily. You will rarely enjoy any long cards in the suit, because declarer will be short in one hand or another and will able to ruff.

There are countless situations where it will cost the defenders a trick if they make the first lead in a suit — in bridge parlance, if they 'break' the suit. Look at this diamond position:

♦ K 10 6 2   ♦ J 7 4   ♦ A 9 5

♦ Q 8 3

If declarer has to play the suit himself, he will lose three tricks in the suit. Suppose he leads the ♦3 from hand towards dummy's ♦J, for example. West will play low, East will win with the ♦A and West will score two further tricks with the ♦K and ♦10.

What will happen if either of the defenders decides to break the suit? His partner will have to play an honor in third seat and declarer will then score a trick with the ♦Q or the ♦J. The defenders cannot afford to break this suit or countless similar suits. Unless declarer will be able to discard his diamond losers, the defenders do best to play a safe suit elsewhere, leaving declarer to lose three diamond tricks later.

One of the most important decisions to make when defending is whether to follow an 'active' or a 'passive' defense. What do these terms mean? An active defense is one where you try to cash tricks or establish tricks that you will be able to cash later. In other words, you attack a new suit despite the risk that this may give away a trick. When instead you follow a passive defense, you make a safe play in a suit where declarer holds all the top cards. You hope that he will have to break the critical suit and thereby lose the maximum number of tricks in it.

Here is a deal that involves the diamond combination that we just saw:

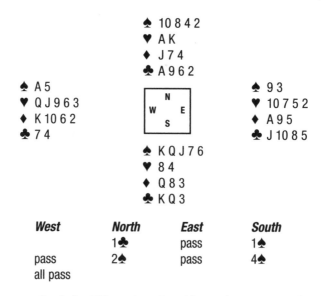

West	North	East	South
	1♣	pass	1♠
pass	2♠	pass	4♠
all pass			

Sitting West, you lead the ♥Q against South's spade game. Declarer wins in the dummy and plays a spade to the king. You win the ace and must consider what to do next. What do you think?

The shrimp fisherman would have little doubt about it. "No tricks for us in hearts," he would say. "Let's try diamonds." The defenders would score the ace and king of diamonds, but declarer would then claim the remaining tricks.

As we saw earlier, if declarer has to play this diamond suit himself, he will lose three tricks in the suit and go down. If you are too 'active' and play diamonds yourself, declarer will lose only two diamond tricks and make his contract for him.

It is often a difficult decision to make, whether to defend actively or passively. On the deal we have just seen, there was no reason to break the diamond suit. It was very unlikely that declarer could discard any diamond losers that he might hold, especially since he hadn't done so before drawing trumps. Since it was much more likely that you would give away a diamond trick if you switched to the suit, it was clear to defend passively, by leading another heart, for example.

Now let's see a deal where you need to defend actively. Take the East cards here:

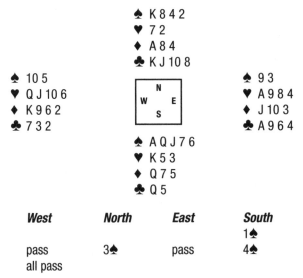

West	North	East	South
			1♠
pass	3♣	pass	4♠
all pass			

West leads the ♥Q and you win with the ♥A, just in case declarer has a singleton ♥K. What is your plan for the defense?

It is unlikely that your partner will win a trick in trumps. Two aces seem to be your allocation in hearts and clubs, so you need two diamond tricks to beat the contract. Can you afford to be passive and wait for your diamond tricks? No, because declarer is threatening to set up dummy's club suit, whether or not he holds the ♣Q. You need to establish your diamond winners before declarer can take any discards on the club suit.

After winning the heart lead, you should switch to a diamond. It doesn't matter which diamond on this deal, but it is best to lead the ♦J (the top of two touching honors). Declarer is now a doomed man. He will probably play low from the South hand, preserving the ♦Q in the hope that West holds the ♣A, in which case the defenders will not then score two diamond tricks. Declarer wins the first diamond with dummy's ace, draws trumps and sets up the clubs. Not good enough! Because of your timely switch to diamonds, you will be able to give partner two diamond tricks when you win with the ♣A. A second round of diamonds through declarer's ♦Q-7 will put the game down one.

What was the difference between the last two deals? On the first one it was unlikely that declarer could discard any diamond losers, so you could afford to defend passively. On the second deal it was very likely that declarer could set up a discard for his diamond losers. It was therefore pretty clear that you had to set up your winners quickly.

Defense is the hardest part of bridge — everyone agrees on that — and sometimes it will be a difficult decision whether you should defend actively or passively. You may have to guess which cards declarer and your partner hold. That's life! The important thing is to realize how expensive it can be if you defend actively at the wrong moment.

To emphasize this message, let's look at some more suit layouts where it will cost you a trick if you break a suit when there is no need to do so.

♦ 10 5 2

♦ Q 9 8 3   ♦ K 7 4

♦ A J 6

If either defender attacks this diamond suit, declarer can score two diamond tricks. Left to his own devices, he will score only one trick in the suit.

♣ 10 6 3

♣ A J 4   ♣ Q 8 7 5

♣ K 9 2

It clearly costs a trick if West leads this club suit, because declarer will make the ♣K. It is equally expensive for East to attack the suit, leading a spot card. Declarer will play low from his hand and West will have to win with the ♣J. Even if West switches elsewhere now, the damage has been done. Declarer can finesse the ♣9 later, forcing West's ♣A and setting up a trick for the ♣K. If declarer has to play the clubs himself, he cannot score a single trick from the suit.

Let's see one more combination:

♣ J 9 4

♣ Q 10 7 2   ♣ K 8 5

♣ A 6 3

If West leads this suit, declarer may play the ♣9 from dummy. This will be covered by the ♣K and ♣A. Declarer can then lead towards dummy's ♣J, establishing a second trick from the suit. If instead he has to play the suit on his own, he can make only one club trick.

Well, you get the idea. It is all too easy to give away a trick when you to make the first lead in a suit. You should therefore be wary about switching to a new suit. Do so only when you think that declarer might dispose of his losers otherwise.

Defending passively may seem an unnatural thing to do, so we will look at one more deal where it is the only way to beat the contract.

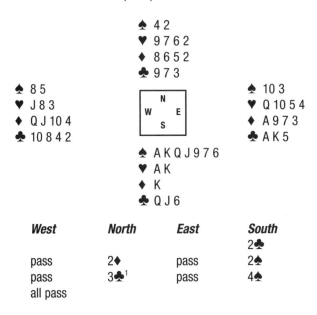

| ♠ 4 2 |
| ♥ 9 7 6 2 |
| ♦ 8 6 5 2 |
| ♣ 9 7 3 |

♠ 8 5   ♠ 10 3
♥ J 8 3   ♥ Q 10 5 4
♦ Q J 10 4   ♦ A 9 7 3
♣ 10 8 4 2   ♣ A K 5

♠ A K Q J 9 7 6
♥ A K
♦ K
♣ Q J 6

West	North	East	South
			2♣
pass	2♦	pass	2♠
pass	3♣[1]	pass	4♠
all pass			

1. Second negative, less than a king.

West leads the ♦Q and, sitting East, you win with the ♦A. The ♦K falls from declarer and you must consider your return. What is it to be?

Many defenders would now play the ♣A 'to see what signal they get from partner'. It makes absolutely no difference how partner signals! By cashing even one club honor, East will give away the contract. Declarer will be able to establish a tenth trick from his remaining ♣Q-J.

Suppose you had been East. What card would you have led to the second trick? Would you choose a low heart? No, because declarer might hold ♥A-K-J; you would have allowed him to take a finesse, even though there was no entry to dummy to perform one himself. There is absolutely no need for you to do anything active in the East seat. You should return a diamond (or a low trump), leaving declarer to try to make a club trick on his own. He will then have no way to make the contract. If he leads the ♣6 at any stage, your partner can win with the ♣10. If instead declarer plays a club honor, you will win with the ♣K and again exit passively with a diamond.

Summary

✓ Making the first lead in a suit costs around half a trick, on average. Be wary of switching around from suit to suit when defending.

✓ There are two main styles of defense. The first is 'active defense', where you break a new suit in an attempt to score tricks or to set them up. The second is 'passive defense', where you refrain from leading a new suit. Instead you play a suit where declarer has all the top cards, leaving the play of the other suits to him.

✓ Deciding whether to defend actively or passively is one of the most difficult aspects of good bridge. When defending a suit contract, you may have to defend actively when there is a strong side suit and declarer is threatening to set up some discards.

ACTIVE DEFENSE OR PASSIVE DEFENSE?

NOW TRY THESE...

1.

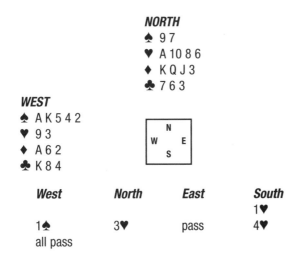

NORTH
♠ 9 7
♥ A 10 8 6
♦ K Q J 3
♣ 7 6 3

WEST
♠ A K 5 4 2
♥ 9 3
♦ A 6 2
♣ K 8 4

West	North	East	South
			1♥
1♠	3♥	pass	4♥
all pass			

You lead the ♠A, East playing the ♠3 and South the ♠6. How will you defend?

2.

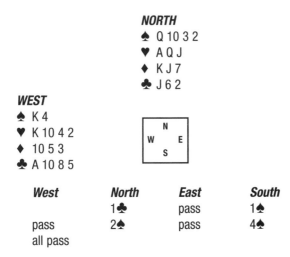

NORTH
♠ Q 10 3 2
♥ A Q J
♦ K J 7
♣ J 6 2

WEST
♠ K 4
♥ K 10 4 2
♦ 10 5 3
♣ A 10 8 5

West	North	East	South
	1♣	pass	1♠
pass	2♠	pass	4♠
all pass			

You lead the ♥2, won with dummy's ♥J; partner plays the ♥3 and declarer the ♥8. Now declarer runs the ♠Q to your ♠K. How will you defend?

3.

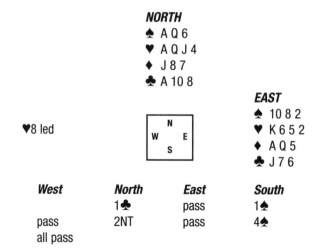

NORTH
- ♠ A Q 6
- ♥ A Q J 4
- ♦ J 8 7
- ♣ A 10 8

EAST
- ♠ 10 8 2
- ♥ K 6 5 2
- ♦ A Q 5
- ♣ J 7 6

♥8 led

West	North	East	South
	1♣	pass	1♠
pass	2NT	pass	4♠
all pass			

Partner leads the ♥8. You win dummy's ♥Q with the ♥K and declarer follows with the ♥9. How will you defend?

4.

NORTH
- ♠ A 6
- ♥ J 7 5 3 2
- ♦ 8 7 4
- ♣ J 7 5

EAST
- ♠ 8 4 3
- ♥ A Q 6
- ♦ A K 10 6
- ♣ 10 8 3

♥10 led

West	North	East	South
			1♠
pass	1NT	pass	4♠
all pass			

Partner leads the ♥10 to your ♥A, the ♥K appearing from South. How will you defend?

ANSWERS

1.

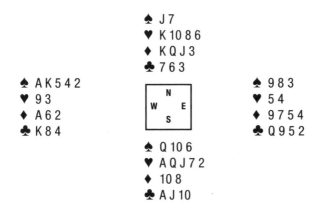

You cash the ♠A, drawing the seven, the three and the six. What next? If you defend passively, exiting with a trump, declarer will draw trumps and set up the diamonds for discards. You will never score a club trick. You can see the threat that dummy's diamonds represent! You must defend actively, switching to the ♣4 at Trick 2. When partner produces the ♣Q, forcing South's ♣A, your ♣K will be the setting trick. If South holds the ♣A-Q, it is unlikely that you could have beaten the contract.

2.

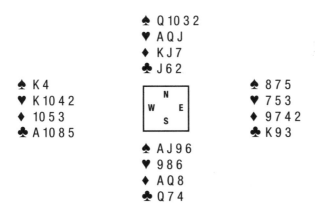

Defending 4♠, you lead the ♥2 to dummy's ♥J. When declarer runs the trump queen to your king, it is dangerous to play a club or a diamond. You should defend passively by returning a spade or a heart. Declarer will eventually lose three club tricks.

3.

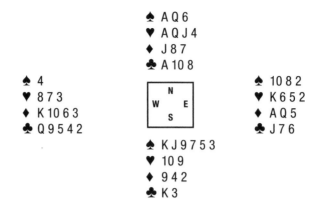

Partner leads the ♥8 against 4♠ and you win dummy's ♥Q with the ♥K, South playing the ♥9. What now? It is fairly clear that your partner has led top of nothing in hearts and that declarer has discards available on the heart suit. If you defend passively, exiting with a trump, declarer will score six spades, three hearts and at least one club trick, making the contract. To defeat the game, you need three diamond tricks. So, defend actively, playing ♦A, ♦Q and another diamond. Down one!

4.

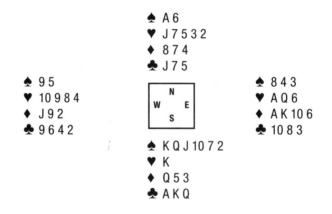

West leads the ♥10 against South's spade game. You win with the ♥A, dropping South's ♥K. Suppose you play the ♦A (or ♦K) next. Partner will discourage with the ♦2, but the damage will have been done. Declarer can win your switch and use the ♠A entry to lead towards the ♦Q. Game made. Instead, you should defend passively by playing a club at Trick 2. Since declarer has only one entry to dummy, he cannot lead twice towards the ♦Q. He will lose three diamond tricks and go down one.

LEAD THE RIGHT CARD IN THE MIDDLE OF THE PLAY

It's choice, not chance, that determines your destiny.

Jean Nidetch

Suppose you decide to switch to a new suit in the middle of the play. Which card should you lead from the suit?

The general rule is that you lead the same card that you would have done when making an opening lead. You lead the top of touching honors and fourth best from other holdings headed by at least one honor. The lead of a high spot card suggests that you have no honor in the suit.

It is important to play the right card in this type of situation:

```
                    ♦ 7 6 3
  ♦ K J 9 4        ┌──────────┐        ♦ 8 5 2
                    └──────────┘
                    ♦ A Q 10
```

Sitting East, you decide to attack this suit in the hope of establishing a trick or two in partner's hand. You must lead the ♦8, to let partner know that you hold no honor. Let's say that declarer plays the ♦10. When your partner wins with the ♦J, he will know that he should not continue the suit from his side of the table. Your lead of the ♦8 places the ♦A-Q in declarer's hand.

Now suppose that the diamond suit lies differently:

♦ 7 6 3

♦ K J 9 4   [□]   ♦ Q 8 2

♦ A 10 5

This time you lead the ♦2, to let partner know that you hold an honor. West wins declarer's ♦10 with the ♦J, as before, but this time he knows that he can safely continue the suit. He returns the ♦4 to your ♦Q, forcing the ♦A. When you regain the lead, you will be able to cash a diamond trick.

Most of the time, then, you lead the same card that you would have done when making an opening lead. You will not be surprised to hear that there are some exceptions to this rule. (Isn't it always the way?) In the next few sections we will look at the most important of these.

Leading an honor when tricks have to be taken quickly

When you are going to switch to a suit where your holding is something like J-5-2 or Q-9-7-3, you will normally lead a low spot card (fourth best from four or more, third best from three). If partner wins the trick, though, he might not find it convenient to continue the suit from his side of the table. Particularly when you are leading through a king, it may work better to lead your honor instead. You will then retain the lead if declarer plays low in second seat.

It's not easy to visualize, so let's look at a sample deal:

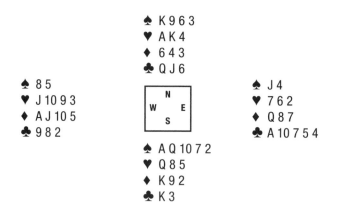

♠ K 9 6 3
♥ A K 4
♦ 6 4 3
♣ Q J 6

♠ 8 5   ♠ J 4
♥ J 10 9 3   ♥ 7 6 2
♦ A J 10 5   ♦ Q 8 7
♣ 9 8 2   ♣ A 10 7 5 4

♠ A Q 10 7 2
♥ Q 8 5
♦ K 9 2
♣ K 3

West, your partner, leads the ♥J against South's spade game. Declarer wins with the ♥A, draws trumps, and leads the ♣K. How will you defend?

Declarer has several entries to dummy, so it cannot help you to hold up the ♣A. How can you possibly beat the contract? You have one trick in clubs and no further tricks in the major suits (partner's lead of the ♥J denied the ♥Q, of course). So, you need three diamond tricks. You cannot afford to exit passively and wait for these tricks. You know that declarer has ten tricks ready to take (five trumps, three hearts and two clubs).

What will happen if you switch to the ♦7? Declarer will breathe a sigh of relief and cover with the ♦9. West will win with the ♦10 and the contract will be safe. West cannot continue diamonds effectively from his side of the table. If he plays a heart or a club instead, declarer will win and discard one of his diamond losers on the third round of clubs.

To beat the contract, you must switch to the *queen* of diamonds. Declarer has no counter. If he plays low, you will remain on lead and can play a second diamond through the king. If instead declarer covers with the ♦K, your partner will score three tricks in the suit. You would make the same lead of the ♦Q from holdings such as ♦Q-8-7-2 or ♦Q-10-2.

Lead the card that will give declarer a guess

Forcing the opponents to guess is a big part of the game. How would you defend with the East cards here?

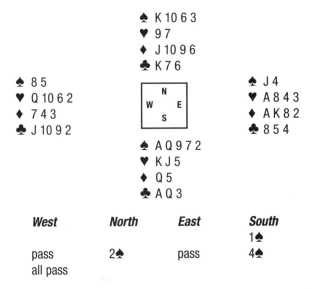

	♠ K 10 6 3		
	♥ 9 7		
	♦ J 10 9 6		
	♣ K 7 6		
♠ 8 5		♠ J 4	
♥ Q 10 6 2		♥ A 8 4 3	
♦ 7 4 3		♦ A K 8 2	
♣ J 10 9 2		♣ 8 5 4	
	♠ A Q 9 7 2		
	♥ K J 5		
	♦ Q 5		
	♣ A Q 3		

West	North	East	South
			1♠
pass	2♠	pass	4♠
all pass			

Declarer wins the ♣J lead with the ♣A and draws trumps with the ace and queen. He then plays the ♦Q to your ♦K. How will you defend in the East seat?

No tricks will come your way in the black suits. Partner will have given you a count signal of the ♦3, so you know you will score a second diamond trick. To beat the contract, you must also score two tricks from the heart suit. What is more, you must attack the suit yourself. If instead you continue to defend passively, playing clubs, declarer will set up the diamond suit and score five trumps, three clubs and two diamonds. Which heart should you lead now, do you think, the ace or a low heart?

You must lead a low heart, giving declarer a guess if he holds ♥K-J-x. If you switch to the ♥A instead, declarer will be spared the guess. He will lose only one heart trick and make the contract easily.

Summary

✓ In the middle of the hand, generally lead the same card that you would have done when making an opening lead. Play the top of touching honors and fourth best from other honor holdings. The lead of a high spot card suggests that you hold no honor in the suit.

✓ When you are leading through a king, or may be doing so, it can pay to lead high from Q-x-x or J-x-x. The intention is to hold the lead if the king is withheld.

✓ When declarer could have a guess to make in the suit, lead a card that will not give away your holding. In particular, lead low from an ace when partner may be able to win the trick with the queen.

LEAD THE RIGHT CARD IN THE MIDDLE OF THE PLAY

NOW TRY THESE...

1.

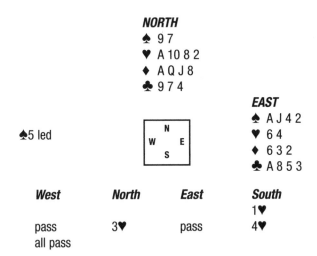

NORTH
♠ 9 7
♥ A 10 8 2
♦ A Q J 8
♣ 9 7 4

♠5 led

EAST
♠ A J 4 2
♥ 6 4
♦ 6 3 2
♣ A 8 5 3

West	North	East	South
			1♥
pass	3♥	pass	4♥
all pass			

Partner leads the ♠5. How will you defend?

2.

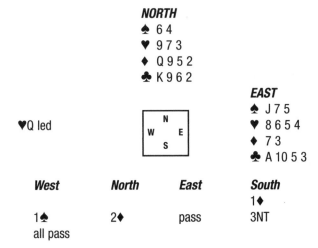

NORTH
♠ 6 4
♥ 9 7 3
♦ Q 9 5 2
♣ K 9 6 2

♥Q led

EAST
♠ J 7 5
♥ 8 6 5 4
♦ 7 3
♣ A 10 5 3

West	North	East	South
			1♦
1♠	2♦	pass	3NT
all pass			

Partner leads the ♥Q against South's 3NT. Declarer wins with the ♥K, crosses to the ♦Q and leads the ♣2. How will you defend?

ANSWERS

1.

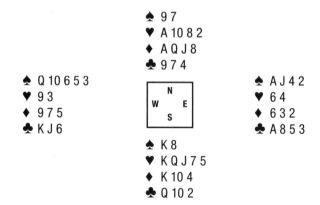

Partner leads the ♠5 against South's game in hearts and you win with the ♠A. You should aim to score four tricks in the black suits. Your best play at Trick 2 is the ♣3. If partner holds the ♣K, you will need two club tricks. By leading a low club rather than ace and another, you may induce declarer to misguess when he holds the king and jack. When South holds the ♣K, as in the diagram, you will need three club tricks. Your lead of a low spot card will tell partner that he should continue to play clubs.

2.

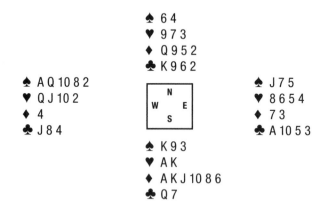

Partner leads the ♥Q against South's 3NT. Declarer wins with the ♥K, crosses to the ♦Q and leads the ♣2. He is trying to steal a ninth trick! Rise with the ♣A and switch to the ♠J, giving partner five spade tricks. If you switch to the ♠5 instead, declarer will play low and survive.

SHOULD YOU COVER AN HONOR LEAD?

 The problem is not that there are problems. The problem is expecting otherwise and thinking that having problems is a problem.

Theodore Rubin

"Always cover an honor with an honor" is a slogan that many beginners quote. It is amazing how many of these easy-to-remember adages are incorrect. If you go through your bridge career always covering when an honor is led, you will lose many more tricks than you gain. Indeed, you would save many hundreds of tricks by following the equally overstated recommendation: "Never cover an honor with an honor."

Cover when you might promote a trick

The purpose of covering is to promote a trick, either for yourself or for your partner. Let's see a position where it is correct to cover.

♦ A J 9 7 2

♦ K 6 4   ☐   ♦ 10 8 5

♦ Q 3

South leads the ♦Q and you cover with the ♦K, won with dummy's ♦A. Your partner's remaining ♦10-8, poised over dummy's ♦J-9-7-2, will now be worth a

---

trick. In other words, East's ♦10 has been promoted. If instead you decline to cover the ♦Q, this card will win the trick. Declarer will subsequently finesse dummy's ♦J and score five diamond tricks.

Let's change the spot cards a bit:

```
                        ♦ A J 10 9 2
        ♦ K 6 4         ┌──────────┐         ♦ 8 7 5 3
                        └──────────┘
                        ♦ Q
```

There would now be no point in covering the ♦Q. Since dummy holds the ♦J-10-9, you cannot possibly promote a spot card in your partner's hand. If you refuse to cover, you will save yourself a trick when (as in the diagram) declarer's ♦Q is a singleton. He will not be able to repeat the finesse. If he subsequently leads the suit from dummy, you will score a trick with the ♦K.

So cover only when it seems possible to promote a trick.

Don't cover when the lead is from touching honors

When an honor lead has been made from the dummy, it is easier to tell whether to cover or not. An important rule to follow is that you should not cover when the lead is from touching honors. Look at this situation:

```
                        ♦ J 10 7 2
        ♦ K 4           ┌──────────┐         ♦ Q 9 8
                        └──────────┘
                        ♦ A 6 5 3
```

Declarer leads the ♦J from dummy. Suppose you 'cover an honor with an honor'. Declarer will win your queen with the ace and lead towards dummy's ♦10 on the next round. He will score three tricks from the suit. Since the ♦J is one of touching honors, you should not cover it. West wins the ♦K and your remaining ♦Q-9 will give you a second trick from the suit.

```
                        ♠ Q J 9 3
        ♠ 10 8 5        ┌──────────┐         ♠ K 6 4
                        └──────────┘
                        ♠ A 7 2
```

With this combination, declarer leads the ♠Q from dummy. If you mistakenly cover with the king, declarer will win with the ace and finesse dummy's ♠9 on the next round. He will score four spade tricks. Since the queen is one of touching honors, you should not cover. The ♠Q will win the trick but declarer will be restricted to a total of only three spade tricks instead of four. If he leads the ♠J on the second round, you will cover with the king to promote West's ♠10.

It was easy to make the right defensive play on the two combinations we have just seen, because the touching honors were on view in the dummy. Let's rotate the last diagram by 180 degrees and imagine that declarer has made the queen lead from his hand:

```
                        ♠ A 7 2
    ♠ K 6 4            ┌─────────┐            ♠ 10 8 5
                        └─────────┘
                        ♠ Q J 9 3
```

When declarer leads the ♠Q, it is again wrong to cover. You cannot actually see that the queen is one of two touching honors, but it is a reasonable assumption to make. If declarer held the ♠Q without the ♠J, he would lead towards the queen instead. (A complete beginner might lead the queen with ♠Q-8-3 opposite ♠A-7-2, it's true. You would then have an amusing story to tell! This doesn't mean that you should misdefend, though, covering with the king, just to cater for such a distant possibility.)

When you hold K-10-x, you can afford to cover a queen led from the closed hand. Even if this does set up a finesse for declarer's remaining J-9, the finesse will lose. Similarly, you can cover from K-9-x, since you can then rule out Q-J-9-x in the closed hand. This will give you some protection against the queen-leading beginner we just mentioned.

Another exception to the rule arises when you hold a doubleton honor:

```
                        ♦ Q J 8 2
    ♦ 10 9 6           ┌─────────┐            ♦ K 4
                        └─────────┘
                        ♦ A 7 5 3
```

When declarer leads the ♦Q in this layout, you do best to cover. If you play low instead, declarer will play the ♦A on the next round, dropping your king, and score all four tricks from the suit.

You cannot be certain that covering is right, however. If declarer holds ♦A-9-7-3, a cover will allow him to run the ♦9 on the second round and score four diamond tricks. If instead you play low, he is more likely to lead the ♦J on the second round in the hope that West began with ♦10-6 and the ♦10 can be pinned. (Why is he likely to guess this way? Precisely because most defenders would cover from K-x.) Still, in the long run it is usually right to cover from a doubleton king in this situation.

Don't cover when you will save declarer a guess

Sometimes declarer needs to guess correctly in a key suit to make his contract. In such a situation, it is important that you not save declarer the guess by covering an honor lead in the suit. Look at this slam deal:

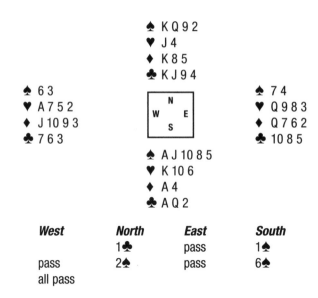

♠ K Q 9 2
♥ J 4
♦ K 8 5
♣ K J 9 4

♠ 6 3
♥ A 7 5 2
♦ J 10 9 3
♣ 7 6 3

♠ 7 4
♥ Q 9 8 3
♦ Q 7 6 2
♣ 10 8 5

♠ A J 10 8 5
♥ K 10 6
♦ A 4
♣ A Q 2

West	North	East	South
	1♣	pass	1♠
pass	2♠	pass	6♠
all pass			

You are sitting East and partner leads the ♦J against South's small slam. Declarer sees that he has a guess to make in the heart suit. He wins with the ♦A and draws trumps with the ace and king. He then leads the ♥J from dummy. If you mistakenly 'cover an honor with an honor', declarer will be spared a critical guess in the suit. The trick will be completed by the king and ace. Declarer can then claim the remaining tricks.

What will happen if you follow with a smooth ♥3 on the first round? Since many of the world's defenders would (incorrectly) cover when they held the queen, declarer is almost certain to place the ♥Q with West. In that case he will rise with the ♥K, hoping that you hold the ♥A. The defenders will then score two heart tricks and beat the slam.

On a deal like this, the moment dummy goes down you must start to think what you will do if the ♥J is led. "Perhaps declarer has a guess in the suit," you will think to yourself. When the moment comes, you will have already rehearsed in your mind the *smooth* play of a low card.

Covering will save declarer a guess in this common situation:

♣ A 10 7 2

♣ Q 6 4

♣ 5 3

♣ K J 9 8

Declarer leads the ♣J from his hand, hoping to 'smoke out' the queen from West. If you cover in the West seat, declarer will be spared a guess and will score four tricks from the suit. If instead you are familiar with the situation and follow *smoothly* with a low card, declarer is likely to place the ♣Q with East. He will rise with dummy's ♣A and finesse East for the missing queen. You will gain two things from not covering: a trick for your ♣Q and the declarer's respect!

This next position is similar. Declarer, who has bid hearts strongly, is playing in some high heart contract. You are East and this is the trump suit:

♥ 6   ♥ J 9 3   ♥ Q 5 4

♥ A K 10 8 7 2

A cunning declarer will lead the ♥J from dummy. With only four trumps out, he has no intention of running the jack. He has led it, just in case you are tempted to 'cover an honor with an honor' from Q-x-x! You know that your partner is short in the suit and that you cannot promote a winner by covering. Play a smooth low card instead and declarer will probably rise with the ace and cash the king.

Don't cover when the finesse cannot be repeated

Sometimes you can see that it will be wrong to cover because declarer cannot repeat the finesse and your honor will live to fight another day. You are West in the following diamond position, and you are defending a notrump contract.

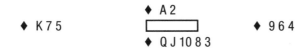

♦ K 7 5   ♦ A 2   ♦ 9 6 4

♦ Q J 10 8 3

When declarer leads the ♦Q from the closed hand, there are two good reasons not to cover. The first is that you expect the queen to be part of touching honors (and you might give away the whole suit when South holds ♦Q-J-9-x-x and would be able to finesse the ♦9 on the second round). The second reason is that declarer will have to play the ♦A on the second round anyway. Keep hold of your ♦K and it will score on the third round.

Summary

✓ The old advice 'always cover an honor with an honor' is wrong more often than not. You should cover only when it seems that you might promote a trick for the defense.

✓ Do not cover one of touching honors. When the lead is made from dummy, you can see whether it is one of touching honors. When the lead is made from the closed hand instead, you may have to assume that declarer would not make such a play unless he held touching honors.

✓ Be particularly wary of covering an honor when this may save declarer a guess in the suit. This particularly applies to covering with a queen. Declarer will not usually lead a jack from his hand unless he can afford (indeed would welcome) a cover with the queen

SHOULD YOU COVER AN HONOR LEAD?

NOW TRY THESE...

1.

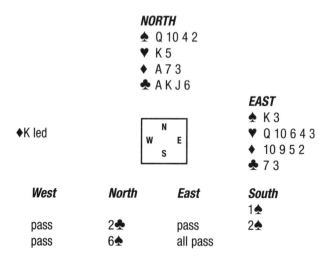

NORTH
♠ Q 10 4 2
♥ K 5
♦ A 7 3
♣ A K J 6

EAST
♠ K 3
♥ Q 10 6 4 3
♦ 10 9 5 2
♣ 7 3

♦K led

West	North	East	South
			1♠
pass	2♣	pass	2♠
pass	6♠	all pass	

West leads the ♦K against 6♠. Declarer wins with dummy's ♦A and leads the ♠Q. Will you cover or not?

2.

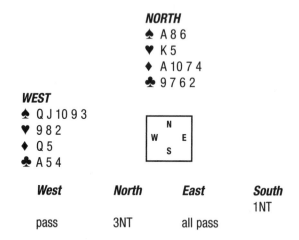

NORTH
♠ A 8 6
♥ K 5
♦ A 10 7 4
♣ 9 7 6 2

WEST
♠ Q J 10 9 3
♥ 9 8 2
♦ Q 5
♣ A 5 4

West	North	East	South
			1NT
pass	3NT	all pass	

You lead the ♠Q against 3NT and South wins with the ♠K. At Trick 2 he leads the ♦J. Will you cover or not?

3.

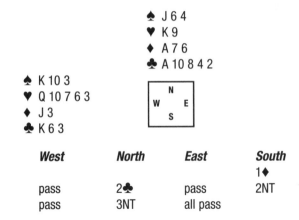

♠ J 6 4
♥ K 9
♦ A 7 6
♣ A 10 8 4 2

♠ K 10 3
♥ Q 10 7 6 3
♦ J 3
♣ K 6 3

West	North	East	South
			1♦
pass	2♣	pass	2NT
pass	3NT	all pass	

You lead the ♥6, partner's ♥J forcing the ♥A. At Trick 2 declarer leads the ♣J. Will you cover or not?

4.

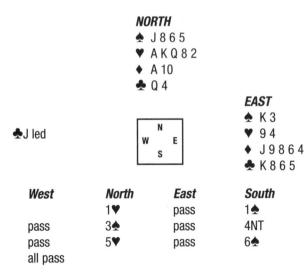

NORTH
♠ J 8 6 5
♥ A K Q 8 2
♦ A 10
♣ Q 4

EAST
♠ K 3
♥ 9 4
♦ J 9 8 6 4
♣ K 8 6 5

♣J led

West	North	East	South
	1♥	pass	1♠
pass	3♠	pass	4NT
pass	5♥	pass	6♠
all pass			

Partner's lead of the ♣J is covered by the queen, king and ace. Declarer leads the ♦Q, overtaking with the ace in dummy, and leads the ♠J from dummy. Will you cover or not?

ANSWERS

1.

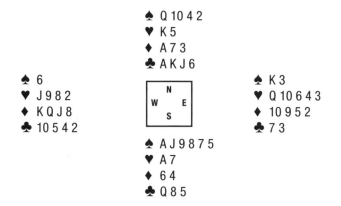

You should not cover. You know declarer probably has at least six trumps, maybe seven; there is no possibility that you could set up a trick for partner by covering the ♠Q. With seven spades, his correct play is the ♠A when you fail to cover (even with only six he may try to drop a singleton king offside). When your ♠K does not fall, he will play four rounds of clubs, hoping to ditch his diamond loser in time. Not today! You will ruff the third club and return a diamond. Down one.

2.

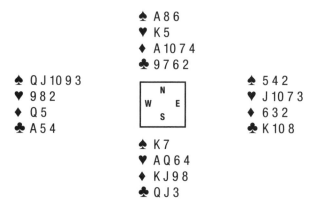

If you cover the ♦J, you will save declarer a guess; he will have nine easy tricks. Play low smoothly and he might rise with the ♦A and finesse through partner into your ♦Q.

3.

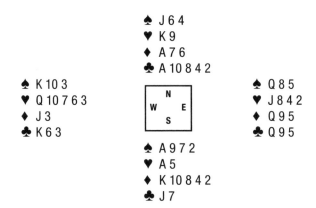

Sitting West, you lead the ♥6 against 3NT. Declarer takes East's ♥J with the ♥A and leads the ♣J. If you fail to cover, your partner will win with the ♣Q. Declarer will win the heart return in dummy, cross to his hand with the ♦K and finesse the ♣10. He will score four club tricks and make the game. Instead, you should cover the ♣J. Partner's ♣Q-9 will be promoted into two tricks and the game will go down.

4.

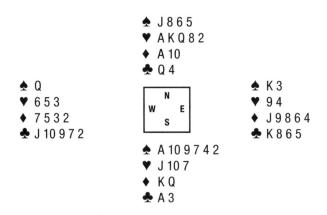

South reaches a small slam in spades and West leads the ♣J, covered by the queen, king and ace. Declarer leads the ♦Q, overtaking with dummy's ♦A, and leads the ♠J from dummy. Will you cover? You should not cover. South may hold seven spades to the A-Q-10 and have no intention of finessing. Another reason not to cover is illustrated in the diagram. Partner may hold a singleton ♠Q! Play the ♠3 instead and declarer will rise with the ♠A. He will then play hearts, hoping to discard his club loser before the defender with the last trump can ruff in. Some hope!

SCORING RUFFS ON DEFENSE

If you don't risk anything, you risk even more.

Erica Jong

Back in Chapter 5 we discussed the merits of leading a singleton against a suit contract. We remarked that a lead from a doubleton is nowhere near as promising; it becomes a better bet when you hold the ace or king of trumps and may therefore have two chances to score a ruff.

Let's look first at deal where the defender in third seat must diagnose whether the opening lead is a singleton or from a doubleton.

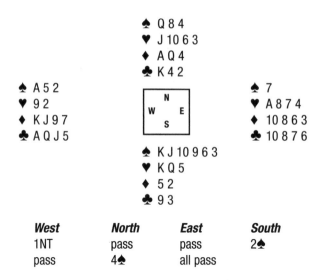

	♠ Q 8 4	
	♥ J 10 6 3	
	♦ A Q 4	
	♣ K 4 2	
♠ A 5 2		♠ 7
♥ 9 2		♥ A 8 7 4
♦ K J 9 7		♦ 10 8 6 3
♣ A Q J 5		♣ 10 8 7 6
	♠ K J 10 9 6 3	
	♥ K Q 5	
	♦ 5 2	
	♣ 9 3	

West	North	East	South
1NT	pass	pass	2♠
pass	4♠	all pass	

You are sitting East and partner leads the ♥9 against South's spade game. What is your plan for the defense?

If partner's ♥9 is a singleton, you will want to win with your ♥A immediately and give him a ruff. If instead he is leading from ♥9-x, you may fare better by holding up the ♥A and planning to win the second round of the suit. Which do you think is the more likely?

The answer, of course, is that partner cannot hold a singleton heart since he opened 1NT! You should therefore hold up your ♥A, signaling encouragement with the ♥8. Declarer wins the trick in the South hand and plays a trump, your partner winning with the ace. After your admirable hold-up at Trick 1, partner can now lead his second heart to your ace. A heart ruff, followed by a club trick, defeats the game.

On some deals, when you hold the ace of the suit led, you will have to guess whether partner's lead is a singleton or part of a doubleton. When in doubt, it is better to assume the lead is a singleton. There are two reasons for this. The first is that a singleton lead is more attractive than a doubleton. The second is that if the lead is from a doubleton and you hold up the ace, declarer may be able to draw trumps anyway.

How can you show partner your entry for another ruff?

Suppose partner leads a singleton diamond and you hold ♦A-9-7-6-2. You win with the ace and return a diamond for partner to ruff. Yes, but *which* diamond should you return? You should choose your spot card to indicate which side suit you would like partner to lead next. A high spot card, the ♦9 here, will ask for the return of the higher remaining side suit. A low spot card, the ♦2, will ask for the lower side suit. With no particular preference you would lead a middle card.

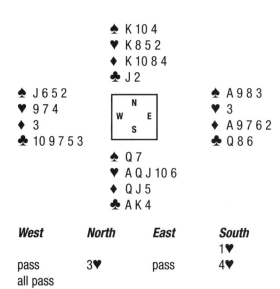

♠ K 10 4
♥ K 8 5 2
♦ K 10 8 4
♣ J 2

♠ J 6 5 2   ♠ A 9 8 3
♥ 9 7 4   ♥ 3
♦ 3   ♦ A 9 7 6 2
♣ 10 9 7 5 3   ♣ Q 8 6

♠ Q 7
♥ A Q J 10 6
♦ Q J 5
♣ A K 4

West	North	East	South
			1♥
pass	3♥	pass	4♥
all pass			

You are sitting East and partner leads the ♦3 against South's game in hearts. Declarer plays low from dummy and you win with the ♦A, declarer playing the ♦5. Which card will you play next?

Since you hold the ♠A as a card of re-entry, you should return the ♦9, your highest spot card in diamonds. Partner will ruff and return a spade to your ace. A second diamond ruff will then put the contract down one.

Suppose you and your partner had never heard of suit-preference signals. When West ruffed the diamond return, he would have to guess whether to play a spade or a club. Half the time he would guess wrongly and the contract would be made.

BY THE WAY

As you continue to learn more about defense, you will discover that suit-preference signals can be useful in many other situations too. However, most of these involve expert-level signaling methods and are beyond the scope of this book.

BY THE WAY

Look again at the diamond suit on this deal. A skilled declarer, suspecting that the lead is a singleton, will attempt to disguise the situation. He will drop the ♦J at Trick 1 (a 'falsecard'), hoping that you read your partner for ♦Q-5-3. On the present deal there is no attractive alternative to a diamond return and you should not be deflected from this path.

Can you signal in the trump suit?

In the introductory chapter we mentioned count signals, where you play high-low to show an even number of cards in a suit that declarer is leading. Somewhat confusingly, it is a universal tradition that playing high-low in the trump suit shows exactly three trumps. This signal, known as a 'trump echo', carries a further meaning: that you are able to take a ruff somewhere. West was grateful for such a signal on this deal:

SCORING RUFFS ON DEFENSE

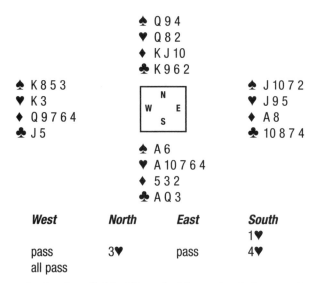

	♠ Q 9 4		
	♥ Q 8 2		
	♦ K J 10		
	♣ K 9 6 2		

♠ K 8 5 3		♠ J 10 7 2
♥ K 3		♥ J 9 5
♦ Q 9 7 6 4		♦ A 8
♣ J 5		♣ 10 8 7 4

	♠ A 6	
	♥ A 10 7 6 4	
	♦ 5 3 2	
	♣ A Q 3	

West	North	East	South
			1♥
pass	3♥	pass	4♥
all pass			

With no attractive lead available, West decides to lead the ♦6. East captures the ♦10 with the ace and returns his remaining diamond, won in the dummy. On the first round of hearts, East should drop the ♥9. This is the beginning of a trump echo, showing three trumps and a desire to ruff. Declarer leads a second round of trumps and West wins with the ♥K, noting that his partner follows with the ♥5 on the second round. Two things are now clear to West: his partner has a third trump and he began with a doubleton diamond. West duly leads a diamond and East ruffs. A subsequent spade trick will defeat the contract.

Ruffing to kill declarer's winner

Another reason to give partner a ruff is to kill a potential winner for declarer. The play may be effective, even if declarer is able to overruff. Let's see an example of that.

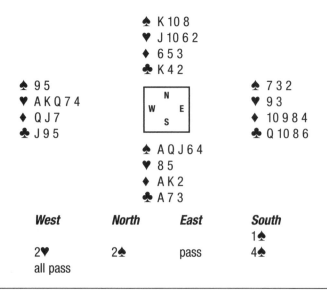

	♠ K 10 8	
	♥ J 10 6 2	
	♦ 6 5 3	
	♣ K 4 2	

♠ 9 5		♠ 7 3 2
♥ A K Q 7 4		♥ 9 3
♦ Q J 7		♦ 10 9 8 4
♣ J 9 5		♣ Q 10 8 6

	♠ A Q J 6 4	
	♥ 8 5	
	♦ A K 2	
	♣ A 7 3	

West	North	East	South
			1♠
2♥	2♠	pass	4♠
all pass			

Sitting West, you lead the ♥A against South's spade game. East signals with the ♥9, indicating a doubleton (or a singleton). When you continue with the ♥K, both closed hands follow. What should you do next?

Suppose your hearts were ♥A-K-x-x-x-x and dummy held Q-J-x. It would be obvious to play a third heart, so that partner could ruff dummy's ♥Q. It would scarcely matter that declarer could overruff, because you would still kill one of dummy's winners. The heart situation on this deal is similar because dummy's ♥J-10 represent a potential trick for declarer. Suppose that you switch to the ♦Q at Trick 3. Declarer will win in his hand and draw trumps, ending in the dummy. He will then run the ♥J, discarding one of his minor-suit losers. When he regains the lead, he will discard his other minor-suit loser on the established ♥10 and make the contract.

To prevent declarer from enjoying a heart winner, you must lead a low heart at Trick 3. Your partner can then ruff dummy's ♥J. It doesn't matter at all that declarer overruffs. You will have destroyed the potential heart trick in dummy and the contract will go down one.

Can you tell from the bidding that partner has a ruff coming?

Before choosing an opening lead, it is important to consider the opponents' bidding, as well as the cards in your hand. When both defenders have shown length in a suit that ends up as a side suit, you can sometimes diagnose a ruff there. That's what happened on this deal:

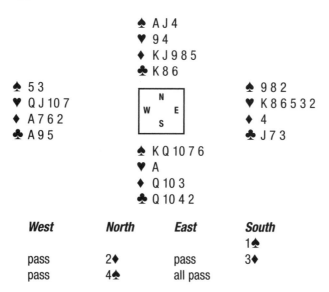

♠ A J 4
♥ 9 4
♦ K J 9 8 5
♣ K 8 6

♠ 5 3
♥ Q J 10 7
♦ A 7 6 2
♣ A 9 5

♠ 9 8 2
♥ K 8 6 5 3 2
♦ 4
♣ J 7 3

♠ K Q 10 7 6
♥ A
♦ Q 10 3
♣ Q 10 4 2

West	North	East	South
			1♠
pass	2♦	pass	3♦
pass	4♠	all pass	

What would you lead from that West hand? Many players would lead the ♥Q without a moment's thought. A solid sequence in an unbid suit? What better lead could there be? You can see what would happen. Declarer would win with the ♥A, draw trumps and eventually score an overtrick — conceding two tricks to the minor-suit aces.

You should look closely at the auction before choosing a lead from the West hand. North has responded in diamonds and South has raised the suit. There is an excellent chance that North-South will hold eight diamonds between them. That leaves East with a singleton! Instead of pushing out an 'autopilot' ♥Q, you should lead the ♦A. When dummy appears with five diamonds, you can be certain that partner has at most one diamond.

What card will you lead at Trick 2? Yes, the *two* of diamonds, your lowest spot card, to suggest a club return. Partner will ruff and return a club. Back on lead with the ♣A, you will deliver a second diamond ruff and beat the contract. "That's unlucky," declarer will say.

Summary

✓ When you are leading a spot card for partner to ruff, play a high spot card to ask partner to return the higher-ranking remaining side suit. Play a low spot card to request the lower-ranking remaining suit.

✓ A high-low signal in the trump suit is called a 'trump echo'. This high-low signal shows *three* cards in the suit (not an even number, as it would do in a side suit). It also tells partner that you can ruff one of the side suits.

✓ It can be worthwhile to get your partner to ruff a potential winner in dummy, even when declarer will be able to overruff.

✓ It is easy to diagnose a potential ruffing situation when you are on lead and have a side-suit singleton. Also look out for situations where you have a long side suit and can judge from the auction that partner may have a singleton or void there.

SCORING RUFFS ON DEFENSE

NOW TRY THESE...

1.

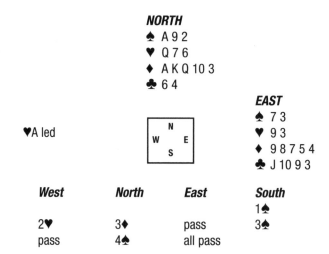

NORTH
♠ A 9 2
♥ Q 7 6
♦ A K Q 10 3
♣ 6 4

EAST
♠ 7 3
♥ 9 3
♦ 9 8 7 5 4
♣ J 10 9 3

♥A led

West	North	East	South
			1♠
2♥	3♦	pass	3♠
pass	4♠	all pass	

Sitting East, you signal with the ♥9 when partner leads the ♥A against the spade game. Partner continues with the ♥K and the ♥J. You ruff the third round of hearts and declarer follows suit. What now?

2.

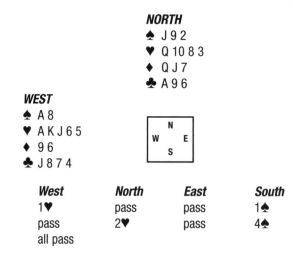

NORTH
♠ J 9 2
♥ Q 10 8 3
♦ Q J 7
♣ A 9 6

WEST
♠ A 8
♥ A K J 6 5
♦ 9 6
♣ J 8 7 4

West	North	East	South
1♥	pass	pass	1♠
pass	2♥	pass	4♠
all pass			

You lead the ♥A, East playing the ♥7 and South the ♥9. What is your plan to beat the contract?

ANSWERS

1.

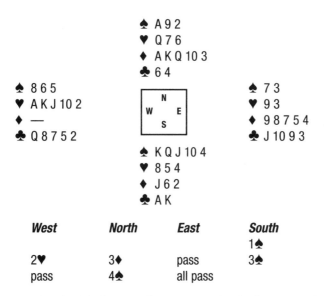

West	North	East	South
			1♠
2♥	3♦	pass	3♠
pass	4♠	all pass	

Sitting East, you signal with the ♥9 when partner leads the ♥A against the spade game. Partner continues with the ♥K and the ♥J. You ruff the third round of hearts and declarer follows suit. What now?

It may seem the most natural thing in the world to switch to the ♣J. Not the best! Declarer will win with the ♣A, draw trumps and claim ten tricks. Look at the card that West chose to lead, to give you your ruff. It was the *jack* of hearts, his highest heart. He is asking you to return a diamond — the higher-ranking remaining suit! So you should return a diamond. Partner ruffs and the game is down one.

2.

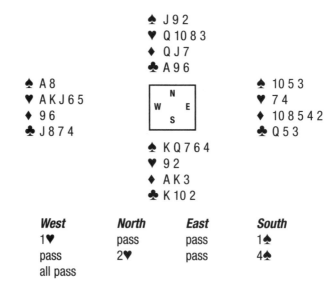

West	North	East	South
1♥	pass	pass	1♠
pass	2♥	pass	4♠
all pass			

Sitting West, you lead the ♥A against South's spade game. Partner plays the ♥7 and declarer plays the ♥9. What now?

Declarer is hoping that after his play of the ♥9 you will place him with no more hearts and that you will switch to a different suit at Trick 2. Your partner would not play the ♥7 from ♥7-4-2, however, so you know that declarer has at least one more heart. You play the ♥K next and everyone follows. How should you continue the defense?

Dummy's ♥Q will be good for a discard, unless you can arrange for partner to ruff it. You should therefore lead another heart at Trick 3. Declarer will finesse the ♥10 and this will be ruffed by East and overruffed by South. When declarer leads a trump, you will leap in with the ♠A and lead yet another heart. Partner can then ruff dummy's ♥Q and the contract will go down.

Defending in this way may seem a bit unnatural. After any other defense, though, declarer will eventually discard a club loser on the ♥Q.

CHAPTER

PRESERVING DEFENSIVE COMMUNICATIONS

 A goal without a plan is just a wish.

Antoine de Saint-Exupery

When you are the declarer, few things are more depressing than finding that you have winners in the dummy but no way to reach them. It is just the same when you are defending. There is not much point in setting up two winners in your hand if you will never have the opportunity to cash them.

In this chapter we will see how you can keep in touch with your partner and ensure that your side scores all the tricks that are due it. We will start with a type of deal that you will encounter time and time again:

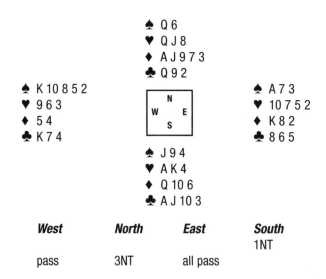

♠ Q 6
♥ Q J 8
♦ A J 9 7 3
♣ Q 9 2

♠ K 10 8 5 2
♥ 9 6 3
♦ 5 4
♣ K 7 4

♠ A 7 3
♥ 10 7 5 2
♦ K 8 2
♣ 8 6 5

♠ J 9 4
♥ A K 4
♦ Q 10 6
♣ A J 10 3

West	North	East	South
			1NT
pass	3NT	all pass	

Sitting West, you lead the ♠5 against 3NT. Your partner wins with the ♠A, you are pleased to see, and returns the ♠7. How will you defend when declarer plays the ♠9?

Let's suppose first that you 'do what comes naturally' and win with the ♠K. Declarer will win the third round of spades with the jack and your partner will then have no spades left. Declarer will take advantage of this by running the ♦Q into the safe hand. The finesse loses but East has no spade to return. The best he can do is switch to a club, but declarer rises with the ace and claims nine tricks.

Winning the second round of spades with the king gives declarer the contract, because it breaks the communications between the defenders. If instead you follow with your ♠2, these spades will then be left:

♠ K 10 8   ♠ —   ♠ 3
                            ♠ J

That's better! When East wins with the ♦K, he still has a spade left to return. You will win the trick with your ♠K and score two more spade tricks to put the contract down one.

Perhaps you are worried that you will sometimes give declarer an undeserved trick if you fail to win when you have the opportunity. If that thought did occur, you are quite right! Let's look at a different deal where you lead from the same spade suit but it would not be a good idea to hold up on the second round.

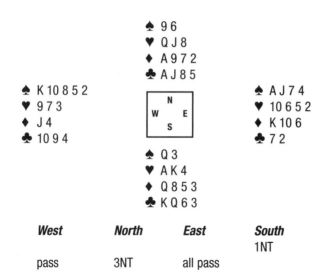

	♠ 9 6		
	♥ Q J 8		
	♦ A 9 7 2		
	♣ A J 8 5		

♠ K 10 8 5 2		♠ A J 7 4
♥ 9 7 3	N	♥ 10 6 5 2
♦ J 4	W E	♦ K 10 6
♣ 10 9 4	S	♣ 7 2

	♠ Q 3	
	♥ A K 4	
	♦ Q 8 5 3	
	♣ K Q 6 3	

West	North	East	South
			1NT
pass	3NT	all pass	

Once again you lead the ♠5 to partner's ♠A. Back comes a low spade and declarer plays the ♠Q. Will you win the trick or not?

You can see from the diagram that this time you need to win with the ♠K. If you duck, declarer will say to himself, "Thanks, you guys!" and run eight more tricks for his contract. So how can you tell whether it is right to win the second round or to hold up? You need to know declarer's spade holding. Does he hold ♠Q-3 (when you should win with the king) or ♠Q-J-3 (when you should hold up)?

The best way you can determine what declarer holds is for your partner to tell you his own holding in the suit. He does this, after winning with his ace, with the card he leads on the second round:

With a doubleton remaining, return the top card
(the 7 from an original holding of A-7-4)

With three or more cards remaining, return the original
fourth-best card (the 4 from A-J-7-4)

By defending in this way, you can tell whether to hold up on the second round. You must look at partner's card and decide if it can possibly be his fourth-best card in the suit. If not, he will have started with three (or two) cards.

Sometimes declarer may try to fool you, but all will become clear if you look at the card that partner returns. Imagine you are West here:

	♠ J 5	
♠ A 9 8 6 2		♠ K 7 3
	♠ Q 10 4	

You lead the ♠6 and partner wins with the ♠K. He returns the ♠7 and declarer plays the ♠Q. Do you win or hold up?

As you can see, declarer has played the ♠Q to fool you! If you win with the ♠A, you will lose touch with your partner. How do you know that declarer started with ♠Q-10-4 and not ♠Q-4? You can tell from the card that partner chose to return. He returned the ♠7, the correct card from an original ♠K-7-3. If declarer had indeed started with ♠Q-4, East would hold ♠K-10-7-3 and in that case he would have returned the ♠3 rather than the ♠7.

Maintaining communications in third seat

It often happens that you have bid a suit during the auction and partner subsequently leads that suit against an opponent's contract in notrump. You may then have to hold up a high card in the third seat to maintain communications with your partner.

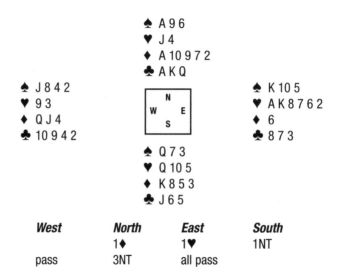

```
                    ♠ A 9 6
                    ♥ J 4
                    ♦ A 10 9 7 2
                    ♣ A K Q

    ♠ J 8 4 2          N            ♠ K 10 5
    ♥ 9 3         W         E       ♥ A K 8 7 6 2
    ♦ Q J 4           S            ♦ 6
    ♣ 10 9 4 2                      ♣ 8 7 3

                    ♠ Q 7 3
                    ♥ Q 10 5
                    ♦ K 8 5 3
                    ♣ J 6 5
```

West	North	East	South
	1♦	1♥	1NT
pass	3NT	all pass	

You are sitting East and partner leads the ♥9 against 3NT, declarer playing the ♥4 from dummy. How will you defend?

Suppose you win with the king and continue with ace and another heart, clearing the suit. Perhaps you hope to gain the lead later, with the ♠K. You will have to wait a long time! Declarer will set up his diamond suit, and when partner wins a diamond trick, he will have no way to reach your hand. Declarer can win whatever West returns and claim nine tricks.

To maintain communications with partner you must make the rather strange play of a spot card at Trick 1. (You will play the ♥8, in fact, to encourage a continuation of the suit later.) Declarer wins with the ♥10 but there is no way for him to make the contract. If he gives your partner a diamond trick, establishing the suit, your partner will still have a heart to play. You will score five heart tricks to put the game down two. You would defend in exactly the same way, playing the ♥8 at Trick 1, if declarer tried to put you off by playing the ♥J from dummy.

Perhaps you are worried that West has a singleton ♥9. It's possible, yes, but in that case there is no way to defeat the contract. Beat most of the contracts that can be beaten and you will become a champion!

Let's see one more deal on this theme:

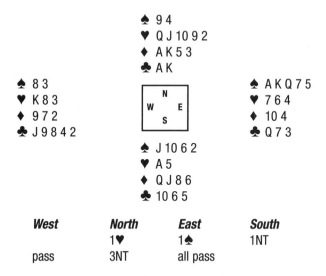

	♠ 9 4	
	♥ Q J 10 9 2	
	♦ A K 5 3	
	♣ A K	

West	North	East	South
	1♥	1♠	1NT
pass	3NT	all pass	

You are sitting East and partner leads the ♠8 against 3NT, declarer playing low from dummy. How will you defend?

How easy it would be to win with the ♠Q and then sit back to consider what plan to make. It would be too late! If you clear the spades next, West will have no spade to play when he wins with the ♥K. If instead you return some other suit, declarer will simply win and establish the hearts, easily making his game.

South has shown a spade stopper with his bid of 1NT over your spade over-call. You can almost 'see' the ♠J-10-x-x in his hand. He is going to make a spade trick anyway and you should let him have it at Trick 1, signaling encouragement with the ♠7. Your partner will then have a spade left. When he wins with the ♥K he will return his remaining spade and you will enjoy four spade tricks to put the game down one!

Protecting the entry to partner's hand

When you and your partner hold one stopper each in declarer's main suit, it is often important that you take these in the right order. You must aim to preserve the entry to the hand that will contain the defensive winners. Here is a straight-forward example of the technique.

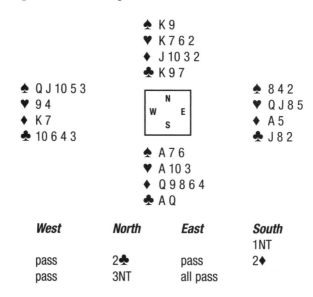

West	North	East	South
			1NT
pass	2♣	pass	2♦
pass	3NT	all pass	

Your partner, West, leads the ♠Q and declarer allows this card to win. (He is hoping that you hold only two spades in the East seat and that he can exhaust your holding.) West plays another spade, won in the dummy, and declarer now leads the ♦J. How will you defend?

You must rise with the ♦A and clear the spades. You hope that partner will have a subsequent entry that will allow him to score his long cards in the suit. On the present deal, declarer cannot score nine tricks without establishing the diamonds. Your partner will win with the ♦K and score two long spades.

See what happens if you play an autopilot 'second hand low'. West wins the first round of diamonds and it will do him no good to clear the spades. He will have no way to gain the lead later and the contract will be made.

Defending in third seat when declarer has a double stopper

When declarer is playing in 3NT and has a double stopper in the suit that you have bid, you may have to defend in a special way to keep in touch with your partner. This type of deal is very common:

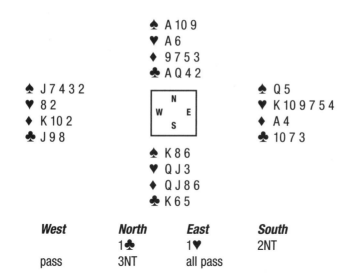

	♠ A 10 9	
	♥ A 6	
	♦ 9 7 5 3	
	♣ A Q 4 2	

♠ J 7 4 3 2		♠ Q 5
♥ 8 2		♥ K 10 9 7 5 4
♦ K 10 2		♦ A 4
♣ J 9 8		♣ 10 7 3

	♠ K 8 6	
	♥ Q J 3	
	♦ Q J 8 6	
	♣ K 6 5	

West	*North*	*East*	*South*
	1♣	1♥	2NT
pass	3NT	all pass	

Once more, you have overcalled in the East seat. Your partner leads the ♥8 and declarer plays low from dummy. How will you defend?

Suppose you win the first trick with the ♥K and return a second round of hearts to dummy's ace. Declarer will be able to set up the diamond suit and make his contract easily. When your partner wins with the ♦K he will have no heart to return.

A better idea is to play the ♥9 at Trick 1, forcing out South's stopper immediately. Now the game will go down. When West wins the first round of diamonds with the king he will have a heart to return and can remove dummy's ♥A. Declarer may delay his fate by cashing four rounds of clubs but you will discard one of your heart winners. You can then win the second round of diamonds and cash three heart tricks to beat the game.

Summary

✓ When you return the suit that partner has led, you lead the top card from a doubleton (i.e. an original three-card holding). From a holding of four or more cards, you return your original fourth-best card. So from A-10-7-5-2 you win with the ace and return the 5.

✓ Suppose you lead the ♠4 from ♠K-8-5-4-2. Partner wins with the ♠A and returns a spade. You must consider holding up your ♠K on the second round, in order to maintain communications. The card that partner returns will help you to decide whether or not to hold up.

✓ When you are in the third seat and partner leads a suit that you have bid, it is often right to allow declarer to win the first round. By doing so, you leave partner with a card in the suit and retain your own top card as an entry.

✓ When the defenders hold one stopper each in declarer's main suit, they must aim to preserve the entry to the hand that will have winners to cash.

PRESERVING DEFENSIVE COMMUNICATIONS

NOW TRY THESE...

1.

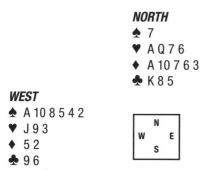

NORTH
- ♠ 7
- ♥ A Q 7 6
- ♦ A 10 7 6 3
- ♣ K 8 5

WEST
- ♠ A 10 8 5 4 2
- ♥ J 9 3
- ♦ 5 2
- ♣ 9 6

West	North	East	South
			1♣
pass	1♦	pass	1NT[1]
pass	2♥	pass	2NT
pass	3NT	all pass	

1. 12-14 HCP.

You lead the ♠5 and partner wins with the ♠K, declarer playing the ♠3. Partner returns the ♠9 and declarer plays the ♠Q. How will you defend?

2.

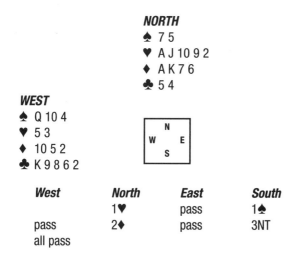

NORTH
- ♠ 7 5
- ♥ A J 10 9 2
- ♦ A K 7 6
- ♣ 5 4

WEST
- ♠ Q 10 4
- ♥ 5 3
- ♦ 10 5 2
- ♣ K 9 8 6 2

West	North	East	South
	1♥	pass	1♠
pass	2♦	pass	3NT
all pass			

You lead the ♣6 and partner plays the ♣Q, won by South's ♣A. Declarer plays a low heart to the jack and East's queen. How will you defend when East returns the ♣7 to South's ♣J?

3.

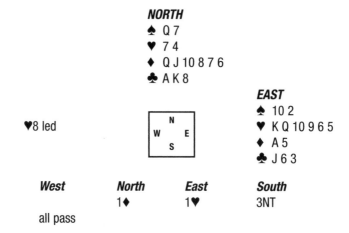

NORTH
♠ Q 7
♥ 7 4
♦ Q J 10 8 7 6
♣ A K 8

EAST
♠ 10 2
♥ K Q 10 9 6 5
♦ A 5
♣ J 6 3

♥8 led

West	North	East	South
	1♦	1♥	3NT
all pass			

Partner leads the ♥8 against 3NT. What is your plan for the defense?

4.

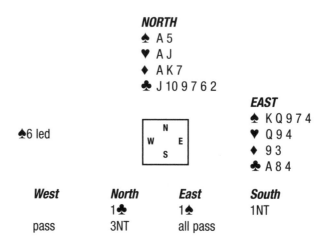

NORTH
♠ A 5
♥ A J
♦ A K 7
♣ J 10 9 7 6 2

EAST
♠ K Q 9 7 4
♥ Q 9 4
♦ 9 3
♣ A 8 4

♠6 led

West	North	East	South
	1♣	1♠	1NT
pass	3NT	all pass	

Partner leads the ♠6 and the ♠5 is played from dummy. How will you defend?

ANSWERS

1.

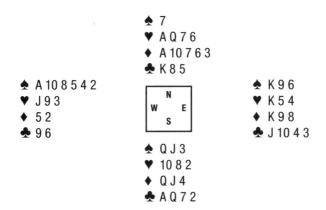

You lead the ♠5 to partner's ♠K. His return of the ♠9, a high card, suggests that he started with three spades and that declarer has ♠Q-J-3. You should therefore hold up your ♠A, allowing declarer to win the second round of spades. Declarer runs the ♦Q, losing to East's ♦K, and (thanks to your hold-up) East has a spade to return. You cash your spade winners to put the game down two.

2.

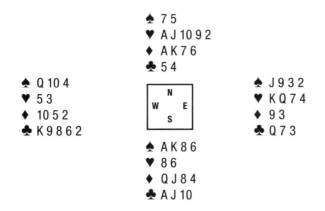

You lead the ♣6 to East's ♣Q and South's ♣A. Declarer runs the ♥8 to East's ♥Q and back comes the ♣7. You can read partner for ♣Q-7-3 (if instead he has ♣Q-7 there is little chance of beating the contract). Duck the second round of clubs. When East wins the next round of hearts, he will have a club to return to you.

3.

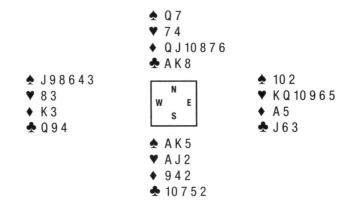

Partner leads the ♥8 against 3NT. Since West would lead low from ♥8-3-2 after your overcall and his failure to raise, you know that declarer has two heart stoppers. What will happen if you play the ♥Q at Trick 1? A skilful declarer will allow this to win. He will capture the next heart and when partner wins with the ♦K he will have no heart to play. Instead you should play the ♥9 at Trick 1, forcing out South's ♥J. Your partner can then win the first round of diamonds and clear the hearts. When you take your ♦A, you will have four heart tricks to cash for down two.

4.

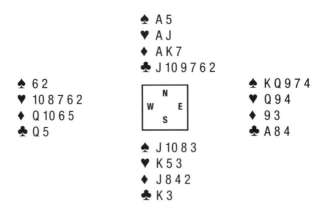

West leads the ♠6 against 3NT and dummy plays the ♠5. The opening lead and the 1NT bid mark South with ♠J-10-x-x. If you win with the ♠Q and return a spade, West will have no spade to play when he wins with the ♣Q. Declarer will set up the clubs and make the contract. Instead you should duck the first round of spades, allowing South to win. If declarer plays the ♣K next, you will duck. West wins the second round of clubs with the queen and clears the spades, defeating the contract.

2

BUILDING A PICTURE
OF THE CLOSED HANDS

ATTITUDE SIGNALS ON PARTNER'S LEADS

 Effective communication is 20% what you know and 80% how you feel about what you know.

Jim Rohn

The traditional method of signaling when partner leads an honor is to play a high card to encourage a continuation (to tell partner that you 'like the suit'). To discourage a continuation, you play a low card. We looked at some basic situations in Chapter 1. When partner leads a side-suit ace against a suit contract such as 4♠, you expect him to hold the king as well. Consequently, you will usually encourage when you hold the queen or when you hold a doubleton and will be able to ruff the third round. With a holding such as J-7-2 or 9-7-6-3, you would play your lowest spot card to discourage a continuation.

Making your signals as clear as possible

As we discussed in the introductory chapter, it does not make much sense to say, "We treat a seven or above as high, a six or below as low." You can only signal with the cards you have been dealt. If you are holding ♠Q-3-2 and want to encourage, you must play the ♠3. An observant partner will note that the ♠2 is missing and consider the possibility that you are encouraging from ♠Q-3-2. Similarly, if you are dealt ♠J-9-8, you will have to discourage with the ♠8 and hope that partner realizes that most of the lower spot cards are on view (in his own hand or the dummy).

That said, you must always make your signal as clear as possible. When you want to encourage, choose the highest spot card that you can afford.

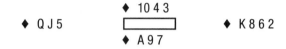

```
                    ♦ 10 4 3
    ♦ Q J 5      ┌──────────┐      ♦ K 8 6 2
                 └──────────┘
                    ♦ A 9 7
```

West leads the ♦Q against a suit contract and, sitting East, you want to give an encouraging signal. Suppose you play the ♦6. Declarer wins with the ace and partner cannot be sure whether you have encouraged. From his point of view, you might hold ♦9-8-7-6, ♦9-8-6, ♦9-7-6, or ♦8-7-6. In any of those cases, it will cost a trick for West to continue diamonds when he regains the lead (declarer will score the ♦K and the ♦10). So, signal clearly with the ♦8 and bring a smile to partner's face. Don't whisper — shout!

What if you want a switch?

When you are deciding whether to encourage partner's lead, don't look just at your holding in that suit alone — consider the whole deal. If you would like a switch to a different suit, you may choose to discourage the first suit regardless of your holding there. Look at this deal, for example:

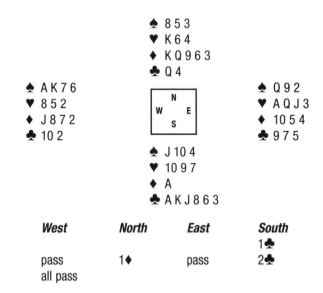

```
                  ♠ 8 5 3
                  ♥ K 6 4
                  ♦ K Q 9 6 3
                  ♣ Q 4
  ♠ A K 7 6                          ♠ Q 9 2
  ♥ 8 5 2           ┌─────┐          ♥ A Q J 3
  ♦ J 8 7 2       W │  N  │ E        ♦ 10 5 4
  ♣ 10 2            │  S  │          ♣ 9 7 5
                    └─────┘
                  ♠ J 10 4
                  ♥ 10 9 7
                  ♦ A
                  ♣ A K J 8 6 3
```

West	North	East	South
			1♣
pass	1♦	pass	2♣
all pass			

You are sitting East and partner leads the ♠A. Holding ♠Q-9-2, you would normally signal encouragement with the ♠9. What good would this do here, though? Suppose partner continues with king and another spade. You win with the queen but cannot play hearts effectively from your side of the table.

Whatever you do next, declarer will score an overtrick.

Now see what happens if you discourage spades by playing the ♠2 on the first trick. Partner's natural switch is a heart, through dummy's king. You win with the jack (the lower of equal cards, making the position clear to partner) and return the ♠9 to his ♠K. A second round of hearts allows you to score two more tricks in the suit. You then surprise partner by producing the ♠Q and the contract is down one.

Signaling when you hold Q-J-x or Q-x

Sometimes partner leads an ace (from ace-king) against a suit contract and your own holding in the suit is headed by the queen-jack:

```
                    ♠ 10 7 6
  ♠ A K 4 2         ┌────────┐        ♠ Q J 8 3
                    └────────┘
                    ♠ 9 5
```

If you wish to offer partner the opportunity to cross to your hand at Trick 2, you should signal with the ♠Q. This signal has a special meaning: it tells partner that you also hold the ♠J (unless the ♠Q is singleton, of course). If he chooses to lead low to your jack on the second round, you may be able to make a damaging switch through declarer's hand. Look at this example:

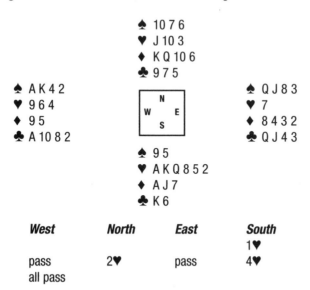

| ♠ 10 7 6 |
| ♥ J 10 3 |
| ♦ K Q 10 6 |
| ♣ 9 7 5 |

```
  ♠ A K 4 2                    ♠ Q J 8 3
  ♥ 9 6 4          N           ♥ 7
  ♦ 9 5         W     E        ♦ 8 4 3 2
  ♣ A 10 8 2       S           ♣ Q J 4 3

                ♠ 9 5
                ♥ A K Q 8 5 2
                ♦ A J 7
                ♣ K 6
```

West	North	East	South
			1♥
pass	2♥	pass	4♥
all pass			

You are sitting East and partner leads the ♠A against South's game in hearts. What signal should you give? You like the spade lead, yes, but suppose you simply encourage with the ♠8. Partner may then continue with king and another spade (which would be the right defense if you held a doubleton spade).

Declarer will ruff the third round of spades and draw trumps. He can then discard one of his club losers on the fourth round of diamonds, making the contract.

A better idea is to signal with the ♠Q on the first trick. Since this promises the ♠J, West will continue with the ♠2 at Trick 2. You win with the ♠J and switch to the ♣Q, through declarer's king. The defenders pick up four speedy tricks in the black suits and that is down one.

Since a signal of the queen carries this special meaning ("I have both the queen and jack"), you cannot play the queen from Q-x. Indeed, in many situations you would not want to waste the queen anyway. Sometimes partner will be able to read what to do, even though you do not encourage from Q-x. Look at this deal:

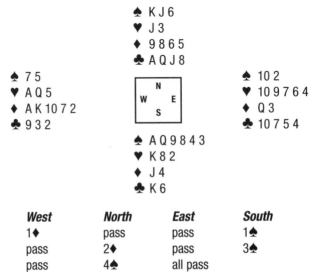

	♠ K J 6	
	♥ J 3	
	♦ 9 8 6 5	
	♣ A Q J 8	

♠ 7 5		♠ 10 2
♥ A Q 5		♥ 10 9 7 6 4
♦ A K 10 7 2		♦ Q 3
♣ 9 3 2		♣ 10 7 5 4

	♠ A Q 9 8 4 3	
	♥ K 8 2	
	♦ J 4	
	♣ K 6	

West	North	East	South
1♦	pass	pass	1♠
pass	2♦	pass	3♠
pass	4♠	all pass	

North's cuebid of 2♦ showed a sound raise in spades. Sitting West, you lead the ♦A against South's spade game. This draws the ♦3 from East and the ♦4 from South. What should you do next?

You must calculate what possible diamond holdings your partner can have. With ♦Q-J-3, he would have signaled with the queen. With ♦J-3, he would have played the jack. So, East must hold either ♦Q-3 or a singleton ♦3. In both cases, a low diamond continuation will give him the lead!

You duly play a low diamond to East's queen and the obvious heart switch gives you two tricks in that suit to put the game down one.

What if your attitude is obvious?

When you cannot beat the card played from dummy, it is usually obvious that you do not hold a high card in the suit. (This does not apply, clearly, when dummy has won with the ace.) Rather than giving a pointless 'discouraging' signal, tell partner something useful — give him a count signal. There are many situations in which this can prove helpful.

◆ QJ5

◆ K 10 8 6 3   [   ]   ◆ 9 7 2

◆ A 4

Partner leads the ♦6 against 3NT and dummy's ♦Q wins. West now knows that declarer holds the ♦A; there is no need for a discouraging attitude signal to tell him this a second time! Instead, give a count signal (here the ♦2, a low card to show an odd number of diamonds).

When West gains the lead, he will continue with a low diamond to dislodge South's bare ace. If instead you had played the ♦9, showing a doubleton, West would place declarer with ♦A-x-x and would know that he could not afford to continue the suit from his side of the table.

Summary

✓ When your partner has led to a trick and you do not have to play high in an attempt to win the trick, you may give an attitude signal. A high card encourages a continuation of this suit; a low card discourages.

✓ When you have a choice of high cards with which to encourage, choose the highest (and therefore clearest) card that you can afford.

✓ When considering whether to encourage, do not look only at your holding in the suit that has been led. If you would prefer partner to switch to a different suit, discourage in the first suit, regardless of what you hold there.

✓ When partner leads an ace and you signal with the queen, this carries a special message that you hold the queen-jack (or a singleton queen). Partner then has the option of leading a low card to the next trick.

✓ When you cannot beat dummy's card (not an ace), your attitude will be obvious to partner. If you could have beaten dummy's card, you would have done so! So give a count signal instead. There are many situations where this will prove useful to your partner.

ATTITUDE SIGNALS ON PARTNER'S LEADS

NOW TRY THESE...

1.

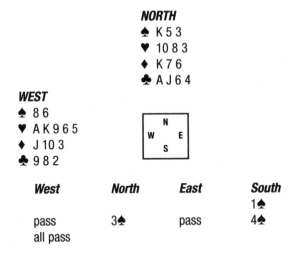

NORTH
- ♠ K 5 3
- ♥ 10 8 3
- ♦ K 7 6
- ♣ A J 6 4

WEST
- ♠ 8 6
- ♥ A K 9 6 5
- ♦ J 10 3
- ♣ 9 8 2

West	North	East	South
			1♠
pass	3♠	pass	4♠
all pass			

Sitting West, you lead the ♥A against South's spade game. Partner plays the ♥4 and declarer the ♥7. How will you continue the defense?

2.

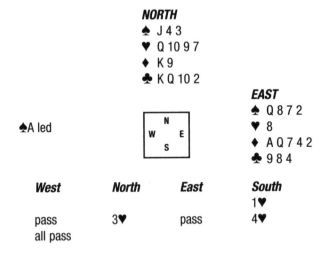

NORTH
- ♠ J 4 3
- ♥ Q 10 9 7
- ♦ K 9
- ♣ K Q 10 2

♠A led

EAST
- ♠ Q 8 7 2
- ♥ 8
- ♦ A Q 7 4 2
- ♣ 9 8 4

West	North	East	South
			1♥
pass	3♥	pass	4♥
all pass			

Your partner leads the ♠A against South's game in hearts. What signal should you make?

ANSWERS

1.

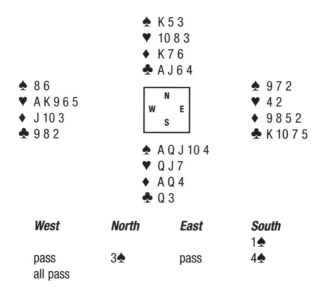

West	North	East	South
			1♠
pass	3♠	pass	4♠
all pass			

Sitting West, you lead the ♥A. Partner plays the ♥4 and declarer the ♥7. Partner's ♥4 appears to be a low card. Is it a discouraging signal, do you think?

Look closely at the missing hearts: the queen, the jack and the two. From a holding of ♥J-4-2, East would discourage with the ♥2. From ♥J-2, he would encourage with the jack.

The only remaining possibilities are ♥Q-J-4 (from which East might have signaled with the ♥Q anyway), ♥Q-4, ♥4-2 and a singleton ♥4. There is a faint chance that partner is trying to get you to switch, probably to a diamond, but if he is, then declarer must have concealed the ♥2. In all these cases, you can afford to continue with the ♥K. As the cards lie, you will note partner's ♥2 on the second round and lead a third heart for him to ruff. The ♣K will be the fourth trick for the defense.

Suppose you do not read the signal correctly and switch to the ♣9 instead. Declarer will rise with dummy's ♣A, draw trumps and make the contract.

2.

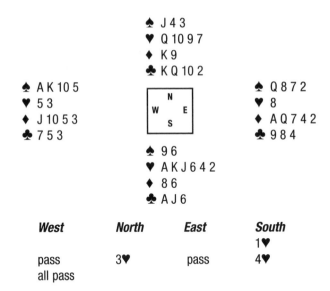

	West	North	East	South
				1♥
	pass	3♥	pass	4♥
	all pass			

Partner leads the ♠A against South's heart game. You are fairly confident that partner is leading from ♠A-K and you hold the ♠Q. Should you therefore signal encouragement with the ♠8? No, because West might then continue with king and another spade (just what you would want him to do if you had started with ♠8-2). Declarer would ruff the third spade, draw trumps and throw a diamond on the clubs, making the contract.

At Trick 1, you should play a discouraging ♠2. West will then switch to the ♦J, allowing you to score two diamond tricks. Finally you will switch back to spades, putting the game down one.

CHAPTER

COUNTING TRICKS
FOR THE DEFENSE

 Do not worry about your difficulties in mathematics. I can assure you mine are still greater.

Albert Einstein

What is your main aim when defending? You won't fall off your chair when you hear the answer. You should aim to beat the contract! (If you play in a match-point pairs event, that's not always true, but we're not going to worry about that in this book.) To keep this target in the front of your mind, you must count the potential tricks available to the defenders as the play proceeds.

Suppose you are halfway through the defense of a major-suit game, for example, and you have already scored two tricks. You must devote all your effort to scoring two more tricks. Ask yourself what card or cards partner can possibly hold that will produce the necessary tricks. "That's obvious!" you may be saying. Maybe, but it is amazing how many defenders are unwilling to make the effort to count anything. Go to this trouble yourself and you will leap ahead of them. Time and again, you will beat contracts that others let make. It's quite an effort to count, yes, but it is worth it.

The defenders need to count their tricks on the following deal.

```
                    ♠ A K 8 7 3
                    ♥ 8 5
                    ♦ 10 6 4
                    ♣ J 10 9
    ♠ J 9 4 2        ┌─────────┐      ♠ Q 5
    ♥ 9 7 2          │    N    │      ♥ A 10 6 4
    ♦ 5              │  W   E  │      ♦ A 9 3 2
    ♣ Q 8 6 5 3      │    S    │      ♣ K 4 2
                     └─────────┘
                    ♠ 10 6
                    ♥ K Q J 3
                    ♦ K Q J 8 7
                    ♣ A 7
```

West	North	East	South
			1♦
pass	1♠	pass	2♥
pass	3♦	pass	3NT
all pass			

You are sitting East, defending 3NT, and your partner leads the ♣5. You cover dummy's jack of clubs with the king and declarer wins with the ace. Declarer plays a diamond to the ten and you win with the ace. When you return the ♣4, West plays the ♣3 and the trick is won in dummy. "Small heart, please," says the declarer. How will you defend?

What is the club situation? West's lead of a low spot card has suggested an honor in the suit. Since he led a fourth-best ♣5 and has since produced the ♣3, he must have started with five clubs. To beat the contract, you must rise with the ♥A and return your last club. Partner will score three club tricks to go with your two red-suit aces and that will be down one.

You may think it was an easy hand to defend. So it was, but a top-class player in the final of the 2005 White House International in Holland failed to rise with the ♥A. Declarer won with the ♥K and claimed nine tricks: four diamonds, two clubs, two spades and a heart. Note also how important it was for West to duck the second round of clubs in order to preserve communications. Since the ♣2 was still missing from his point of view, there was every chance that East was returning his middle card from an original ♣K-4-2.

On the next deal East can beat 3NT provided he stops to *think*, rather than simply following general guidelines.

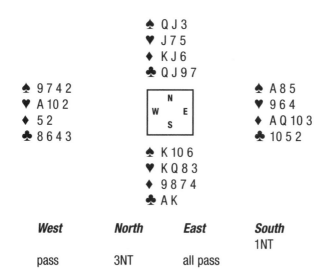

| ♠ Q J 3 |
| ♥ J 7 5 |
| ♦ K J 6 |
| ♣ Q J 9 7 |

♠ 9 7 4 2		♠ A 8 5
♥ A 10 2		♥ 9 6 4
♦ 5 2		♦ A Q 10 3
♣ 8 6 4 3		♣ 10 5 2

| ♠ K 10 6 |
| ♥ K Q 8 3 |
| ♦ 9 8 7 4 |
| ♣ A K |

West	North	East	South
			1NT
pass	3NT	all pass	

You are sitting East and partner leads the ♠7 (second best from four low). Declarer plays low from dummy. What is your plan for the defense?

Partner's lead of a high spot card tells you that there is no future in spades. Suppose you win the spade lead with the ace. Which suit should you switch to? An inexperienced player would probably recall some general rule about 'leading up to weakness in the dummy' and switch to the ♥9. This will not beat the contract. Partner has room for only one ace or king in his hand (there are 19 points missing and declarer's 1NT showed 15-17 points). Suppose partner holds the ace or king of hearts and wins with this card at Trick 2. At best he will switch to a diamond, allowing you to score two tricks in the suit. That is only four tricks for the defense and declarer will claim the remainder.

All the time you must ask yourself, "How can we score enough tricks to beat the contract?" On the present deal you must aim for these five tricks: the ♠A, three diamond tricks and one winner in partner's hand. At Trick 2, you must switch to the ♦3, even though it is a lead into dummy's strength. Do you see the point of this play? Your ♦A-Q-10 will then be poised over dummy's remaining ♦K-J. If your partner subsequently gains the lead with a high heart *or* a high club, the contract will go down! On the present layout, declarer will have only seven tricks after winning the diamond switch cheaply. When he plays a heart, your partner will win with the ♥A and return a diamond.

Counting defensive tricks can be just as important in a suit contract. Let's see an example of that.

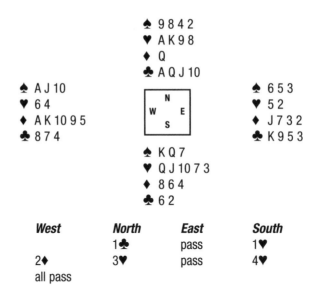

	♠ 9 8 4 2	
	♥ A K 9 8	
	♦ Q	
	♣ A Q J 10	

♠ A J 10		♠ 6 5 3
♥ 6 4		♥ 5 2
♦ A K 10 9 5		♦ J 7 3 2
♣ 8 7 4		♣ K 9 5 3

	♠ K Q 7	
	♥ Q J 10 7 3	
	♦ 8 6 4	
	♣ 6 2	

West	North	East	South
	1♣	pass	1♥
2♦	3♥	pass	4♥
all pass			

Sitting West, you lead the ♦A against South's heart game. How will you continue the defense?

Dummy has a singleton diamond, so one trick is your limit in that suit. Where can you find three more tricks? There are two main possibilities. Partner may hold ♠K-x-x, in which case you could switch to the ♠J and collect three tricks in the suit. The other chance is that partner holds the ♣K instead of the ♠K (he cannot have both). In that case you may be able to score two spade tricks and one club trick, to go with the diamond trick already scored. Do you see how to do this? You need to switch to the ♠J at Trick 2. Declarer will probably win with the ♠K, draw trumps with the ace and queen and take a club finesse. Your partner wins with the ♣K and returns a spade through South's remaining ♠Q-7. You collect two spade tricks and the game is down one.

Some players use 'suit-preference signals' at Trick 1 when it is clear that no further tricks are available in the suit that has been led. Here East would follow with the ♦2 on the first trick, playing his lowest spot card to indicate something useful in clubs (the lower-ranking of the two remaining suits). You still have to *think* in the West seat! Suppose you treat partner's signal as a command to play a club at Trick 2. Although the club finesse will lose to East's ♣K, you will make only one spade trick, with the ace, and declarer will throw his spade loser on a good club.

You have to remember that the object of a signal is tell partner what you hold. It does not tell him what to do! Partner must calculate that himself, bearing in mind both your signal and the cards in his own hand. On this deal, you have to think to yourself: "It looks like partner has the ♣K. In that case I had better switch to the ♠J to give us a chance of two tricks in that suit."

Summary

✓ When you are defending, always keep in mind the main objective —
beating the contract. Ask yourself, "What card or cards can partner
hold that will allow us to defeat the contract?"

✓ One of the most important tasks for a defender is counting. You
count high card points, to help you place the high cards. You count
suit lengths, to allow you to determine the shape of declarer's hand.
You also count potential tricks, both for declarer and for the defense.
Counting may seem like hard work, particularly when you do it for
the first time. It is worth the effort!

COUNTING TRICKS FOR THE DEFENSE

COUNTING TRICKS FOR THE DEFENSE

NOW TRY THESE...

1.

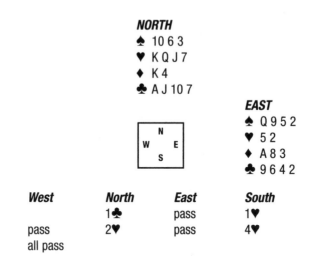

NORTH
♠ 10 6 3
♥ K Q J 7
♦ K 4
♣ A J 10 7

EAST
♠ Q 9 5 2
♥ 5 2
♦ A 8 3
♣ 9 6 4 2

West	North	East	South
	1♣	pass	1♥
pass	2♥	pass	4♥
all pass			

West leads the ♦Q, covered by dummy's ♦K. How will you defend with the East cards?

2.

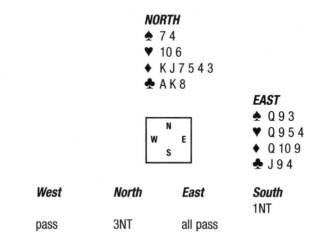

NORTH
♠ 7 4
♥ 10 6
♦ K J 7 5 4 3
♣ A K 8

EAST
♠ Q 9 3
♥ Q 9 5 4
♦ Q 10 9
♣ J 9 4

West	North	East	South
			1NT
pass	3NT	all pass	

West leads the ♠2 against 3NT and declarer wins your queen with the king. He cashes the ♦A and plays a second diamond, partner discarding the ♣2. How will you defend when declarer plays the ♦J from dummy?

ANSWERS

1.

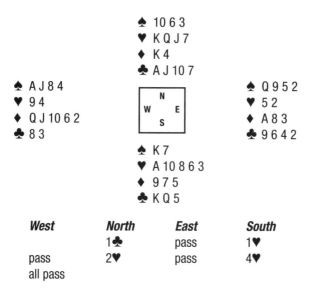

```
                    ♠ 10 6 3
                    ♥ K Q J 7
                    ♦ K 4
                    ♣ A J 10 7
  ♠ A J 8 4                        ♠ Q 9 5 2
  ♥ 9 4           N                ♥ 5 2
  ♦ Q J 10 6 2  W   E              ♦ A 8 3
  ♣ 8 3           S                ♣ 9 6 4 2
                    ♠ K 7
                    ♥ A 10 8 6 3
                    ♦ 9 7 5
                    ♣ K Q 5
```

West	North	East	South
	1♣	pass	1♥
pass	2♥	pass	4♥
all pass			

West leads the ♦Q, covered by dummy's ♦K. How will you defend on the East cards?

Suppose you win with the ♦A and 'return partner's suit'. The contract will be made. West wins the second round of diamonds and cannot play spades effectively from his side of the table. If he plays ace and another spade, declarer will make an undeserved trick with the ♠K. If instead West exits with a trump or a club, declarer will draw trumps and throw one of his spades on dummy's fourth club.

What must you do, in the East seat, in order to defend effectively? Yes, you must count the defenders' potential tricks! You can see two tricks in diamonds. It is unlikely that the defenders will score any tricks in hearts or clubs, so two tricks will be needed from the spade suit. In case declarer has the ♠K, which can only be attacked from your side of the table, you must switch to the ♠2 at Trick 2. This will give the defense four tricks: two spades and two diamonds. You may beat the contract even if South holds ♠K-J. In that case he will have to guess which honor to play.

2.

```
                  ♠ 7 4
                  ♥ 10 6
                  ♦ K J 7 5 4 3
                  ♣ A K 8
   ♠ J 10 6 2          ┌─────────┐          ♠ Q 9 3
   ♥ A J 8 3          │    N    │          ♥ Q 9 5 4
   ♦ 8               │ W     E │          ♦ Q 10 9
   ♣ 10 6 3 2         │    S    │          ♣ J 9 4
                     └─────────┘
                  ♠ A K 8 5
                  ♥ K 7 2
                  ♦ A 6 2
                  ♣ Q 7 5
```

West	North	East	South
			1NT
pass	3NT	all pass	

West leads the ♠2 against 3NT and, sitting East, you play the ♠Q, won by South's ♠K. Declarer cashes the ♦A and plays another diamond, West discarding the ♣2. Declarer calls for dummy's ♦J and you win with the ♦Q. What now?

It is possible that your partner led from ♠A-J-8-2 or ♠A-10-8-2 and that you can take three spade tricks by returning the ♠9 now. However, you need five tricks to beat the game and three plus one does not equal five! Partner led the ♠2, so you know that he started with only four spades. What is more, if partner does hold the ♠A, declarer surely has the ♥A and will therefore have at least nine tricks at his disposal.

By counting the potential tricks available to the defenders on a spade return, you can tell that such a defense cannot succeed. You must hope instead for four heart tricks. Since you may need to lead hearts through more than once, the card to lead is the ♥Q. When partner holds ♥A-J-x-x, as you must hope, this thoughtful switch will defeat the contract. Notice that leading the ♥4 would not be good enough: declarer simply plays low from his hand, and partner cannot continue hearts from his side.

CHAPTER

CLUES FROM THE BIDDING

We can learn even from our enemies.

Ovid

Do you think you would defend better if you knew where all the cards were? Of course you would! That's why a skilled defender puts so much effort into building a picture of the closed hands. How can this be done?

Let's think first about determining the shape of the hidden hands. During the play, you will get information every time someone shows out of a suit. Your partner will also assist you by giving count signals. In this chapter we will consider the information that comes from a different source — the opponents' bidding. Suppose declarer opened 1♠ and rebid 2♥, for example. He is probably 5-4 in those suits. If you lead the ace and king of diamonds and declarer ruffs the second round, you will already be close to placing him with 5-4-1-3 shape.

Now let's consider high-card points. Suppose the opponents' bidding is: 1♥-1♠; 2♥-4♥. The opener has shown a minimum hand, by rebidding 2♥, and will usually be close to the 12-14 point range. If dummy goes down with 12 points and you hold 10 yourself, you will mentally place your partner with around 4-6 points. If he shows up with an ace, early in the play, you will base your future plans on the assumption that he holds at most a queen outside.

How can you work out what declarer has?

Let's look at a typical deal where you can reconstruct most of declarer's hand by referring to the bidding.

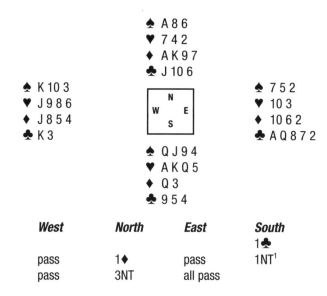

West	North	East	South
			1♣
pass	1♦	pass	1NT[1]
pass	3NT	all pass	

1. 12-14 HCP.

Sitting West, you lead the ♥6 to East's ♥10 and declarer's ♥K. You cover the ♠Q, because you hold the ♠10 as well as the ♠K, and the trick is won by dummy's ♠A. Declarer then runs the ♠8 to your ♠10. How will you defend from this point?

South's 1NT rebid showed 12-14 points. The fact that your partner could produce no heart higher than the ten at Trick 1 tells you that declarer holds the ♥A-K-Q. You can also place him with ♠Q-J. So that is 12 points, and he can hold at most one more queen. If declarer holds the ♣Q, you are unlikely to beat the contract. Dummy's diamonds are immune from attack and declarer will be able to set up a club trick to bring his total to nine. You should therefore mentally assign the ♣Q to your partner, alongside the ♣A that you already know he must hold. You switch to king and another club and the contract goes down two. If you fail to switch to a club, persisting with hearts instead, declarer will breathe a sigh of relief and collect his nine top tricks.

On the next deal it is a 1NT opening that allows you to calculate the high cards that declarer must hold and therefore the limited possibilities left for your partner's hand.

```
                    ♠ A K 7 3
                    ♥ 7 4
                    ♦ K J 9 7
                    ♣ 9 6 4

     ♠ J 2            ┌─────┐          ♠ 10 9 6
     ♥ 9 8 6 2        │  N  │          ♥ Q J 10 3
     ♦ 10 5 4 2      │W   E│          ♦ 8 6
     ♣ A K 3          │  S  │          ♣ Q 8 7 2
                      └─────┘
                    ♠ Q 8 5 4
                    ♥ A K 5
                    ♦ A Q 3
                    ♣ J 10 5
```

West	North	East	South
			1NT
pass	2♣	pass	2♠
pass	4♠	all pass	

South opens a 15-17 point 1NT and West, your partner, leads the ♣A against the eventual contract of 4♠. You encourage with the ♣8 and he continues with king and another club to your queen, South following suit. A good start to the defense, yes, but how will you continue?

If you don't give this much thought, the routine action is to switch to the ♥Q. It is easy to calculate what will happen next. To make up a minimum of 15 points, declarer must hold the ♥A-K and the ♦A. He has already shown the ♣J (bringing his total to 12) and will make the contract whatever combination of queen and jacks he holds in spades and diamonds. If he holds the ♠Q-J, he will draw trumps and finesse the ♦J (ruffing his heart loser if he is 3-3 in the red suits). Holding the ♠J and ♦Q instead, he will drop your partner's ♠Q and score ten tricks without the need of a ruff. The same ten tricks will be available when he holds the ♠Q and ♦Q. So a heart switch cannot defeat the contract. What can you do instead?

You must play a fourth round of clubs, deliberately giving a ruff-and-sluff. When partner holds the ♠J, which will still leave South with a sound 16-count, partner will ruff with that card and force one of dummy's trump honors. The setting trick will then come from your ♠10-9-6. We will look further at the subject of promoting extra trump tricks in Chapter 22. For now, just remember that when all else looks bleak, leading the thirteenth card in a suit can have surprising results.

Sometimes you hold most of the defensive cards yourself. It is then relatively easy, when dummy goes down, to judge which little gem in partner's hand might give you a chance to defeat the contract. You are West on the next deal:

```
                        ♠ J 9 3
                        ♥ Q 6 4
                        ♦ J 10 8 7
                        ♣ A K 9
    ♠ A Q 7 2                            ♠ 10 5 4
    ♥ 10 9 7          ┌──────────┐       ♥ J 8 3 2
    ♦ A K 5          N│    N     │        ♦ 6 4 2
    ♣ 6 4 3        W │ W      E  │ E      ♣ 8 7 2
                     │    S     │
                     └──────────┘
                        ♠ K 8 6
                        ♥ A K 5
                        ♦ Q 9 3
                        ♣ Q J 10 5
```

West	North	East	South
			1NT
pass	3NT	all pass	

You lead the ♦A against 3NT and partner plays a discouraging ♦2. The dummy is strong, with a full 11 points. Add that to South's minimum of 15 points and you see that your partner can hold at most a jack. What chance is there of beating the contract?

Defenders who do not bother to count points might switch to the ♥10 at this stage. It is all too easy to predict the outcome: declarer will win the heart switch and establish the diamond suit, eventually scoring three hearts, two diamonds and four clubs.

To beat the contract, you need to score three spade tricks to go with the ♦A-K. You should therefore switch to a low spade at Trick 2. There are now two ways in which the contract might go down. When the cards lie as in the diagram, declarer is put to an awkward guess. To make the contract he will have to rise with dummy's ♠J. If instead he plays low from dummy, hoping that you hold ♠A-10-x-x, he will go down. East's ♠10 will force the king and you will score three spade tricks when declarer seeks to establish the diamonds.

The second way in which the contract might go down is if declarer started with ♠K-x. In that case he will have no play for the contract, whatever he does on the first round of spades. Winning with the ♠J would not help him at all because your ♠A would drop the ♠K on the second round and you would again score three spade tricks to go with the two top diamonds.

Summary

✓ When you get your first look at dummy, you should add the points that it contains to the points that declarer has suggested by his bidding. This will allow you to estimate the points held by your partner.

✓ Suppose your partner can hold at most 2 points. Place him with the specific queen or jack that will give you the best chance of beating the contract and then defend accordingly.

✓ Do not make 'automatic' plays on defense, such as continuing partner's suit or switching to a Q-J-10-x combination. Instead, stop and make a plan to defeat the contract. Sometimes a count of declarer's points will tell you that the automatic defense cannot possibly succeed.

CLUES FROM THE BIDDING

NOW TRY THESE...

1.

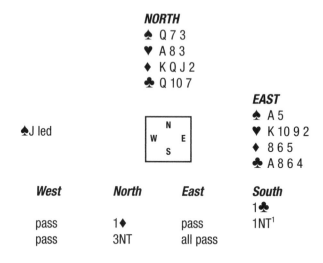

NORTH
♠ Q 7 3
♥ A 8 3
♦ K Q J 2
♣ Q 10 7

♠J led

EAST
♠ A 5
♥ K 10 9 2
♦ 8 6 5
♣ A 8 6 4

West	North	East	South
			1♣
pass	1♦	pass	1NT[1]
pass	3NT	all pass	

1. 12-14 HCP.

West leads the ♠J against 3NT and the ♠3 is played from dummy. Sitting East, what is your plan for the defense?

2.

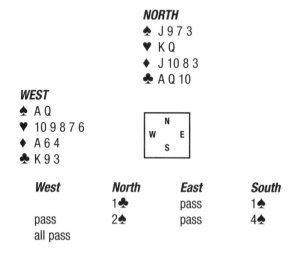

NORTH
♠ J 9 7 3
♥ K Q
♦ J 10 8 3
♣ A Q 10

WEST
♠ A Q
♥ 10 9 8 7 6
♦ A 6 4
♣ K 9 3

West	North	East	South
	1♣	pass	1♠
pass	2♠	pass	4♠
all pass			

You lead the ♥10, won in the dummy with the ♥K, and declarer runs the ♠9 to your ♠Q. What is your plan for the defense?

ANSWERS

1.

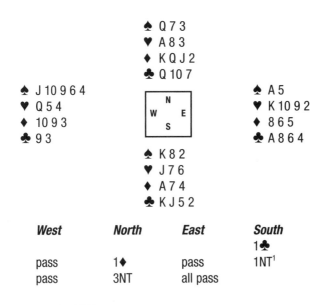

West	North	East	South
			1♣
pass	1♦	pass	1NT[1]
pass	3NT	all pass	

1. 12-14 HCP.

West leads the ♠J against 3NT and the ♠3 is played from dummy. Sitting East, what is your plan for the defense?

South's 1NT rebid showed 12-14 points and you can see 25 points between your own hand and the dummy. This leaves a maximum of 3 points (including the ♠J) in the West hand. You know for sure that South holds the ♠K and there cannot be any future for the defense in the spade suit. Can you see a chance anywhere else?

The only real chance is that West will hold the ♥Q-x-x(-x). So, rise with the ♠A and switch to the ♥10. There is no way for declarer to make the contract after this accurate defense. He will no doubt win the third round of hearts with the ace and turn nervously to the club suit. He was right to be worried! You will win with the ♣A and cash a long heart to put the contract down one.

2.

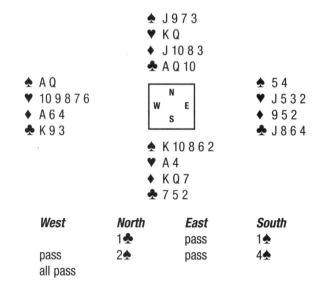

♠ J 9 7 3
♥ K Q
♦ J 10 8 3
♣ A Q 10

♠ A Q
♥ 10 9 8 7 6
♦ A 6 4
♣ K 9 3

♠ 5 4
♥ J 5 3 2
♦ 9 5 2
♣ J 8 6 4

♠ K 10 8 6 2
♥ A 4
♦ K Q 7
♣ 7 5 2

West	North	East	South
	1♣	pass	1♠
pass	2♠	pass	4♠
all pass			

Sitting West, you lead the ♥10 against game in spades. Declarer wins in the dummy and runs the ♠9 to your ♠Q. What now?

South's leap to game suggests at least 11 points. You cannot therefore expect your partner to hold more than a queen or a jack. You can see three defensive tricks in your own hand and the best chance to add a fourth trick is to find partner with the ♣J. In that case you must attempt to establish a club trick before declarer sets up a discard on the diamond suit. You must switch to the ♣3 at Trick 3!

Declarer cannot survive this thrust. If he finesses the ♣10, East will score the ♣J and your two aces will put the game down one. Suppose instead that declarer finesses the ♣Q successfully and plays a second round of trumps. You win with the ♠A and persist with a second round of clubs. Declarer can win and set up the diamonds but there will be a club trick to cash when you win with the ♦A.

(It doesn't assist the defense on this particular deal, but what signal do you think East should give in hearts at Trick 1? It is obvious when dummy's ♥K wins the trick that East does not hold the ♥A. Rather than confirming this fact with a discouraging attitude signal, East should give a count signal. He should play the ♥5, the second-best card from four. This is more likely to be from four cards than two, so West can place declarer with a doubleton ace in the suit. If East had instead played the ♥2, West would place declarer with ♥A-x-x. *When you cannot beat dummy's card, give a count signal.*)

CHAPTER

THE RULE OF ELEVEN

 One has to be able to count if only so that at fifty one doesn't marry a girl of twenty.

Maxim Gorky

Why do most players like to lead their fourth-best card from a useful suit, instead of (say) the third-best card or any low card? It's because it will help partner to read how the suit lies. For example, when partner leads a two, you can deduce that he holds only four cards in the suit. (The two is his fourth-best, so he cannot possibly hold a fifth-best card!)

In this chapter we will look at the famous Rule of Eleven, which is a clever trick that can be used by the partner of the opening bidder. Here it is:

> **Subtract the value of the card led from 11. This will tell you how many higher cards the other three players hold between them.**

Let's see a couple of examples before we investigate what practical use it can be. Suppose partner leads the ♦6 against 3NT and the suit lies like this:

♦ J 9 3

♦ K 10 8 6 4   ♦ A Q 7   ♦ 5 2

Sitting East, you subtract the value of the card led (6) from 11. The answer is five, which means that the North, South and East cards contain five cards higher than the six between then. Dummy holds two of them and you hold none at all. So, you know that declarer holds three cards higher than the six.

Try the next example for yourself. You are sitting East.

♠ Q 10 8

♠4 led   ♠ ???   ♠ A 9 5

Partner leads a fourth-best ♠4 against some notrump contract. How many cards does declarer hold in spades that are higher then the four?

Take 4 from 11 and you get the answer 7. You can see three cards higher than the four in dummy and you hold three more yourself. So declarer can hold only one card higher than the four. Easy!

How does the Rule of Eleven help you read declarer's holding?

When the Rule of Eleven tells you that declarer has only one higher card in the suit led and he has already won the first trick with that card, you will know that he has no further stopper in the suit. Look at this deal:

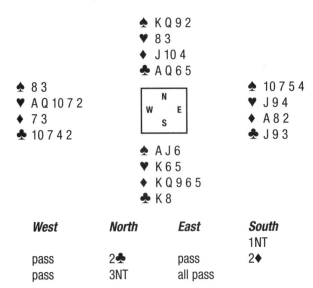

♠ K Q 9 2			
♥ 8 3			
♦ J 10 4			
♣ A Q 6 5			

♠ 8 3   ♠ 10 7 5 4
♥ A Q 10 7 2   ♥ J 9 4
♦ 7 3   ♦ A 8 2
♣ 10 7 4 2   ♣ J 9 3

♠ A J 6
♥ K 6 5
♦ K Q 9 6 5
♣ K 8

West	North	East	South
			1NT
pass	2♣	pass	2♦
pass	3NT	all pass	

West leads the ♥7 against 3NT. You play the ♥J and declarer wins with the ♥K. Declarer crosses to the ♠K and leads the ♦J. How should you defend? Perhaps it seems to you that declarer is planning a finesse against the ♦Q and that you should play low to allow partner to win with that card. If you do play low, declarer will quickly score nine tricks. With one trick from each red suit in the bag, he will add another seven top winners in the black suits.

The Rule of Eleven tells you that declarer has only one heart higher than the seven in his hand; this is the king, which you have already seen. You should therefore rise immediately with the ♦A and return a heart, defeating the contract. Note that since West must hold the ace and queen of hearts, declarer must hold the king and queen of diamonds, to make up at least 15 points for his 1NT opening. So there can be no point in holding up the ♦A.

How can the Rule of Eleven help you know what card to play at Trick 1?

Occasionally, the Rule will tell you that declarer cannot beat the card that has been led. In that case you may be able to play low from your own hand, allowing partner to make a further lead through dummy's honor. Look at this deal:

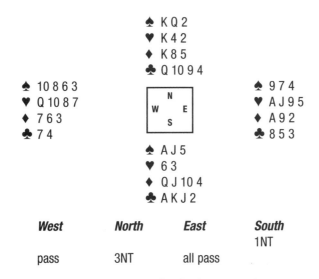

	♠ K Q 2	
	♥ K 4 2	
	♦ K 8 5	
	♣ Q 10 9 4	

West		East
♠ 10 8 6 3		♠ 9 7 4
♥ Q 10 8 7		♥ A J 9 5
♦ 7 6 3		♦ A 9 2
♣ 7 4		♣ 8 5 3

	♠ A J 5	
	♥ 6 3	
	♦ Q J 10 4	
	♣ A K J 2	

West	North	East	South
			1NT
pass	3NT	all pass	

You are sitting East and your partner leads the ♥7 against 3NT. You subtract 7 from 11 and discover that the other three hands hold four cards higher than the ♥7. You can see one in the dummy and three in your own hand. So declarer cannot beat the seven and must hold ♥ 6-3!

You contribute the ♥5 from your hand and West's ♥7 wins the trick. He continues with another heart through dummy's king and the defenders score four hearts and the diamond ace to beat the game. Had you played any higher heart on the first trick, the contract would have been made.

How do you use the Rule of Eleven to read the opening lead?

The Rule of 11 can sometimes help you to read whether partner has led from strength or weakness. You are East here:

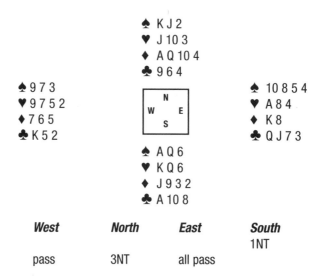

West	North	East	South
			1NT
pass	3NT	all pass	

West leads the ♥7 against 3NT and you win with the ace, declarer playing the ♥6. What now?

If partner has led from strength in the heart suit, it may well be right to continue hearts. Can this be the case, though? Apply the Rule of 11 to the opening lead and you will find that there should be *four* cards higher than the seven in the other three hands. (This is on the temporary assumption that the ♥7 is a fourth-best lead.) You can see four such cards between your own hand and the dummy, which leads to the conclusion that declarer holds none at all.

However, it is not possible that your partner holds ♥K-Q-9-7, because this would leave a maximum of 14 points available for declarer's strong 1NT. You are therefore forced to conclude that West's ♥7 lead is a high spot card from a weak suit (either 9-7-5-2 or 7-5-2). If you continue hearts, declarer will have time to set up the diamonds and make the contract easily. Instead you must switch to clubs, hoping that partner holds the ace or king. When the cards lie as in the diagram, this defense will beat the contract. When declarer takes a losing diamond finesse to your king, you will be able to score a total of three clubs, one heart and one diamond.

Summary

✓ The Rule of Eleven states: subtract the spot card led from 11 and the result will tell you how many cards the three remaining hands hold that are higher in rank.

✓ You can use this Rule to assess the strength, or otherwise, that declarer holds in the suit. Sometimes you will be able to tell that he has only one stopper in the suit; on other occasions you will be able to deduce that he is strong in the suit. In either case, you can choose your play at Trick 1 or Trick 2 accordingly.

✓ Sometimes application of the Rule will allow you to tell that the lead is not a fourth-best card but a lead from a weak suit. In that case you will probably want to switch elsewhere when you gain the lead.

THE RULE OF ELEVEN

NOW TRY THESE...

1.

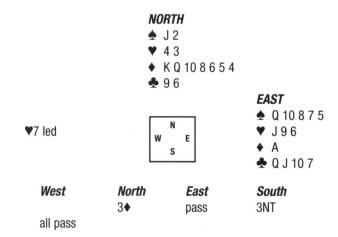

NORTH
♠ J 2
♥ 4 3
♦ K Q 10 8 6 5 4
♣ 9 6

EAST
♠ Q 10 8 7 5
♥ J 9 6
♦ A
♣ Q J 10 7

♥7 led

West	North	East	South
	3♦	pass	3NT
all pass			

West leads the ♥7 against 3NT. You play the ♥J and declarer wins with the ♥A. He leads the ♦J, partner following with the ♦7, and you win with the ♦A. How do you read the lie of the heart suit? What is your plan for the defense?

2.

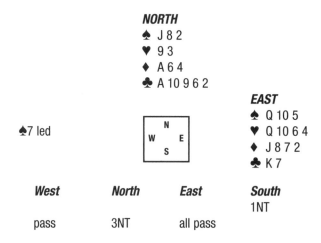

NORTH
♠ J 8 2
♥ 9 3
♦ A 6 4
♣ A 10 9 6 2

EAST
♠ Q 10 5
♥ Q 10 6 4
♦ J 8 7 2
♣ K 7

♠7 led

West	North	East	South
			1NT
pass	3NT	all pass	

You are sitting East and partner leads the ♠7 against 3NT. The ♠2 is played from dummy and your ♠10 is won by declarer's ♠A. At Trick 2 declarer runs the ♣Q to your ♣K. How do you read the lie of the spade suit? How will you defend from this point?

ANSWERS

1.

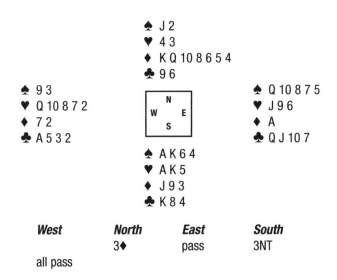

West	North	East	South
	3♦	pass	3NT
all pass			

West leads the ♥7 against 3NT. You play the ♥J and declarer wins with the ♥A. He leads the ♦J, partner following with the ♦7, and you win with the ♦A. How do you read the heart suit? What is your plan for the defense?

The Rule of 11 tells you that declarer started with two hearts higher than partner's lead of the seven. So declarer might (in theory) hold ♥A-K-x, ♥A-Q-x, ♥A-10-x, ♥A-8-x, or ♥A-7-x. You can rule out A-Q-x, because he would then have won the first trick with the queen. And if his second-best card is no better than the ten it is very likely that he would have held up the ace for a couple of rounds. So it is a near certainty that declarer began with the ace and king of hearts. In that case, there is no future in a heart continuation; declarer surely has enough tricks set up to make the contract.

At Trick 3 you should switch to the ♣Q, which represents your best chance of scoring four tricks in a hurry. When the cards lie as in the diagram, this effort will be rewarded. The defenders will indeed score four clubs tricks, beating the contract.

Note that declarer did not play to his best advantage on the first trick. Since he would welcome a heart continuation, as opposed to a club switch, he should have won the first round of hearts with the king instead of the ace. Since declarer would not hold up the king from K-x-x (the defenders might then run the whole suit), East could draw no inference that declarer held the ace as well as the king. He might well decide to continue hearts, allowing the contract to make.

2.

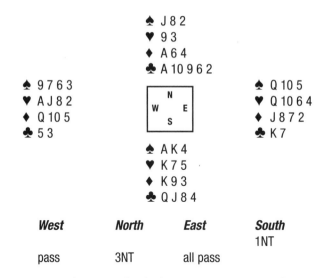

	West	North	East	South
				1NT
	pass	3NT	all pass	

You are sitting East and partner leads the ♠7 against 3NT. The ♠2 is played from dummy and your ♠10 is won by declarer's ♠A. At Trick 2 declarer runs the ♣Q to your ♣K. How will you defend from this point?

Apply the Rule of Eleven and it tells you that the other three hands should contain four spades higher than the seven. You can see four such cards in your own hand and the dummy; if the lead is a fourth-best card, declarer will have no card higher than the seven. In other words, West has led from ♠A-K-9-7-(x). This possibility can be discounted when declarer wins the first trick with the ace. Your Rule of 11 math has not worked, which means that partner did not lead his fourth-best spade. Indeed, you are now forced to assume that partner's spade lead was from weakness.

When declarer takes a club finesse, losing to your king, you need to seek four tricks in a hurry. If you mistakenly persevere with spades, returning the queen, you will not only allow declarer to score enough tricks for the contract, but you will also give him an extra trick in the spade suit. The best chance of beating the contract is to switch to hearts. Which card in hearts should you play? If you lead the ♥4, declarer will run this to dummy's ♥9 and survive; West will not be able to continue hearts effectively when he wins the trick. Instead you should switch to the ♥Q — an unusual play that is necessary because you are on lead for what is probably the last time (you have no more entries in your hand). This switch will net four tricks in the suit and game will be down one.

COUNT SIGNALS ON LEADS BY DECLARER

 We can have facts without thinking, but we cannot have thinking without the facts.

John Dewey

As we mentioned in the introductory chapter, we do not give attitude signals (high to encourage, low to discourage) when declarer makes the first lead in a suit. Whether you want the suit to be played or not, declarer is already playing it! It is much more useful to give count signals (high to show an even number of cards in the suit; low to show an odd number). Indeed, this is a popular treatment wherever bridge is played. Sometimes such signals help partner directly with his play in the suit led. On other occasions they merely help him to build up a complete picture of the hand.

Can a count signal help partner's hold-up?

Count signals are invaluable when declarer is playing a long suit in dummy and your partner has to judge when to take his ace. Look at this deal:

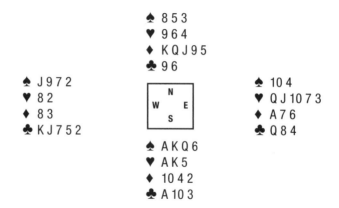

After a 2NT-3NT auction you lead the ♣5 from the West seat and are pleased to see partner produce the ♣Q. Declarer holds up his ♣A for two rounds, winning the third round of clubs. He then leads the ♦2 to dummy's ♦K. Your partner knows that South holds at least two diamonds, because he opened 2NT. It is therefore obvious to hold up the ♦A on the first round. What should he do when declarer continues with the ♦Q from dummy?

Since dummy has no outside entries, East wants to take his ♦A on the round that includes declarer's last diamond. If declarer started with three diamonds, East needs to hold up his ♦A until the third round. If declarer started with only two diamonds, East does not want to hold up again because doing so would allow declarer to score two diamond tricks — possibly enough for the contract. How can East tell how many diamonds declarer has?

The answer is that you, in the West seat, must tell your partner how many diamonds you hold. On this deal you will play the ♦8 on the first round of the suit, showing an even number of diamonds. East will then know that declarer holds three (or possibly four) diamonds, and will hold up his ace. He will refuse to take the ♦A on the second round too, restricting declarer to two diamond tricks, and the contract will go down one.

Let's change the deal a bit to see what might happen when South holds only two diamonds. The full layout might then be:

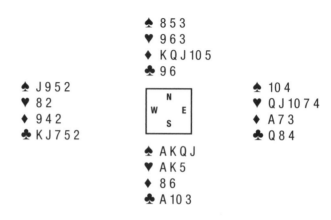

Once again you lead the ♣5 and declarer holds up the ♣A until the third round. He leads the ♦6 to dummy's king, East holding up, and continues with the ♦Q. If East holds up for a second time on this layout, declarer will score nine tricks — four spades, two hearts, two diamonds and one club.

However, since you now hold three diamonds in the West seat you will give a different count signal. You will play the ♦2, your lowest spot card, to show an odd number of diamonds. East will then be able to place you with three diamonds and declarer with two. When South has only two diamonds, it is essential on this deal to take the ♦A on the second round, restricting him to only one diamond trick. East does indeed play his ♦A on the second round of the suit, just as declarer is running out, and the contract goes down one.

What if declarer falsecards?

A skilful declarer will sometimes attempt to disguise his length in a suit, hoping to gain assistance from the defenders. When he attempts this deception, you can often rescue your partner by giving a count signal. Let's look at a typical example.

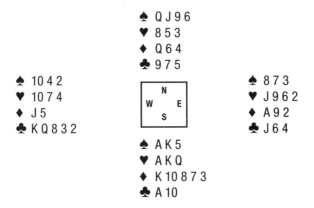

```
              ♠ Q J 9 6
              ♥ 8 5 3
              ♦ Q 6 4
              ♣ 9 7 5
♠ 10 4 2                      ♠ 8 7 3
♥ 10 7 4         N           ♥ J 9 6 2
♦ J 5        W     E          ♦ A 9 2
♣ K Q 8 3 2      S           ♣ J 6 4
              ♠ A K 5
              ♥ A K Q
              ♦ K 10 8 7 3
              ♣ A 10
```

You are sitting East after an auction of 2♣-2♦; 2NT-3NT. Partner leads the ♣3 and declarer wins immediately with the ♣A (a hold-up cannot break the defenders' communications because West's lead of the ♣3 indicates at most a five-card suit). Declarer cashes the ace and king of spades and leads the ♦K from his hand. How will you defend in the East seat?

Perhaps it seems to you that declarer started with a doubleton ♠A-K and is seeking an entry to the two spade winners in dummy. (This is exactly the illusion that he is trying to create.) If declarer does indeed hold no more spades, it might well be good defense to hold up your ♦A, aiming to prevent declarer from using the ♦Q as an entry to dummy and the isolated ♣Q-J there. Here, however, a hold-up in diamonds will prove disastrous. One diamond trick is all that declarer needs to make the contract!

There is a way that you can tell how the cards lie. When declarer cashes the ace and king of spades, your partner must give you a count signal, playing the ♠2 and then the ♠4. You can then place West with three spades, leaving declarer with three spades also. The deception is exposed! You will capture the first round of diamonds and return a club. West turns up with four club tricks and you beat the contract.

Should you always give count?

You should give a true count signal only when you judge that partner may find it useful. Whenever declarer may have a guess to make in a suit, play your cards upwards regardless of your length. Do not help declarer to read how the cards lie. This is a typical example:

	♦ A Q 7	
♦ 8 5	□	♦ J 9 4 3
	♦ K 10 6 2	

Declarer begins by playing the ace and queen of diamonds. On the third round he will have to guess whether to finesse the ♦10 or play for the drop. Of course, it would be unwise (we are tempted to use a less sympathetic word) for one or both defenders to give the position away by signaling an even number of cards in the suit. Left to his own devices, declarer will have a difficult guess to make.

Summary

✓ When declarer plays a suit, the defenders should usually give a count signal.

✓ Count signals are particularly important when declarer is playing a suit in an entry-less dummy. By signaling his own length, a defender can let his partner know how many cards declarer holds in the suit. The other defender can then judge when to take his ace.

✓ When declarer is trying to disguise his own length in a suit, a count signal by one defender may allow his partner to figure out the situation.

✓ Do not give a count signal when this may help declarer to guess correctly in the suit.

COUNT SIGNALS ON LEADS BY DECLARER

NOW TRY THESE...

1.

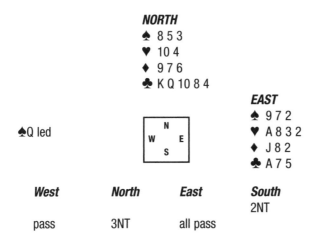

NORTH
♠ 8 5 3
♥ 10 4
♦ 9 7 6
♣ K Q 10 8 4

EAST
♠ 9 7 2
♥ A 8 3 2
♦ J 8 2
♣ A 7 5

♠Q led

West	North	East	South
			2NT
pass	3NT	all pass	

Declarer wins with the ♠A and leads the ♣J, which wins. He continues with a club to dummy's ♣K. How can you tell whether to win this trick?

2.

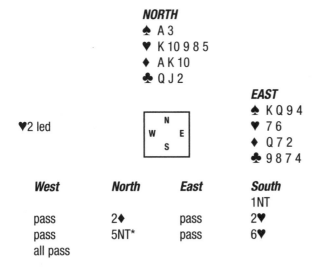

NORTH
♠ A 3
♥ K 10 9 8 5
♦ A K 10
♣ Q J 2

EAST
♠ K Q 9 4
♥ 7 6
♦ Q 7 2
♣ 9 8 7 4

♥2 led

West	North	East	South
			1NT
pass	2♦	pass	2♥
pass	5NT*	pass	6♥
all pass			

The 5NT bid meant 'pick a slam' — either 6♥ or 6NT. Declarer plays the ♥A-K and cashes three clubs, all following. He then throws you in with ace and another spade, dropping the ♠J from his hand. How will you know what to do next?

ANSWERS

1.

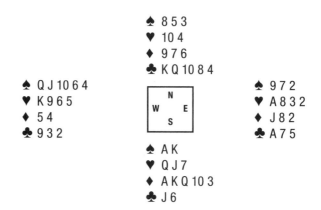

In 3NT, declarer wins the ♠Q lead and plays the ♣J. You allow this to hold and he continues with the ♣6 to dummy's ♣K. Everything depends on West's count signal in clubs. If he plays low-high, indicating that declarer has two clubs, you win the second round of clubs. You then clear the spades, beating the contract. If instead West plays high-low in clubs, leaving South with three clubs, you will hold up the ♣A twice.

2.

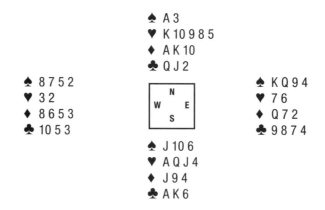

In 6♥, declarer wins the trump lead, draws trumps and scores three club tricks. He then plays the ♠A and the ♠3 to your ♠Q, dropping the ♠J. If declarer began with two spades, another spade would give him a ruff-and-sluff; in that case, you would have to play a diamond in the hope that West held the ♦J. However, West's high-low in spades tells you that you can exit safely with the ♠K and later score a trick with the ♦Q.

CHAPTER

CHOOSING A HELPFUL DISCARD

The more alternatives, the more difficult the choice.

Abbé D'Allanival

How many times after a defense has gone wrong have you heard someone say: "But you asked for a spade!" It is a common misconception that when you makes your first discard, you are telling partner what suit to play next. That is not the purpose of discards, or of any type of signal. Whatever discard or signal you make, you are merely giving partner information about your hand. He must then work out what to do by adding this to information from other sources — his own hand, the opponents' bidding and the play so far. How could you possibly tell partner what to do when you cannot see what cards he holds?

Suppose it's your partner who makes a discard and he tells you he holds something useful in hearts. You should not say to yourself, "Partner wants me to switch to hearts." Rather, you should think, "Partner holds a high heart. Armed with that knowledge, how should I defend?"

Understand that concept and you will have taken a big step towards becoming a good defender!

What does a discard tell you?

Our recommended method of discarding is the traditional one of throwing a high card to show strength in that suit or a low card to show lack of interest. Do not think, however, that you must *always* send a telegraph informing the world which high card you hold. Suppose you have to make a discard from ♥Q-9-6-3 and ♦8-7-5-2. On most deals it will not help partner at all if you throw the ♥9 to indicate a heart honor. It is much more likely that this information will assist the declarer. So instead you would normally discard the ♦2, suggesting no special interest in diamonds.

Let's look at a deal where you do need to tell partner where your strength is:

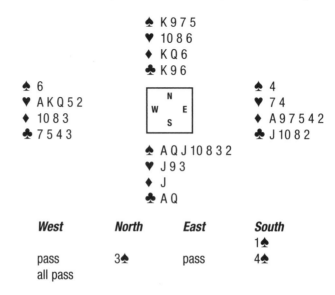

	♠ K 9 7 5	
	♥ 10 8 6	
	♦ K Q 6	
	♣ K 9 6	

♠ 6		♠ 4
♥ A K Q 5 2		♥ 7 4
♦ 10 8 3		♦ A 9 7 5 4 2
♣ 7 5 4 3		♣ J 10 8 2

	♠ A Q J 10 8 3 2	
	♥ J 9 3	
	♦ J	
	♣ A Q	

West	North	East	South
			1♠
pass	3♠	pass	4♠
all pass			

West, your partner, scores the first three tricks with the ace, king and queen of hearts. What discard will you make on the third round of hearts?

You will throw the ♦9, a high diamond to indicate a high card in diamonds. West will then switch to a diamond, giving you the setting trick. Without a helpful discard from you, West would have to guess which suit to play next. If he happened to play a club (or a trump), declarer would discard his diamond loser on the third round of clubs and make the contract.

Did you notice another possibility? You might have ruffed partner's winner on the third round of hearts in order to play the ♦A yourself. Although this would work as the cards lie, it might misfire if declarer held

♠A Q J 10 8 3 ♥9 7 3 ♦— ♣A 7 5 3

He could then ruff the ♦A and take two club discards on the ♦K-Q.

What if you can't afford to throw a high card?

It may seem obvious but you should not throw away a card that might prove useful later in the play. Suppose you hold ♣K-10-9-7 and would like to tell partner that you have something good in clubs. It is quite possible that you cannot afford to throw the ♣10. In such a situation you should throw a low card in some other suit. It is more important to keep the right cards in your hand than to use them to pass some message to your partner.

Look at this deal, which features that very club holding:

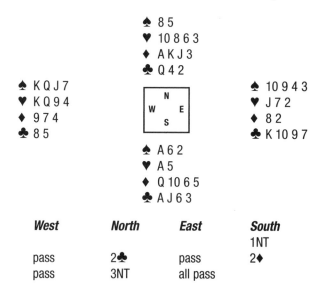

West	North	East	South
			1NT
pass	2♣	pass	2♦
pass	3NT	all pass	

Your partner, West, leads the ♠K against 3NT. Declarer wins the third round of spades, throwing a heart from dummy, and plays three rounds of diamonds. What discard will you make from the East seat?

There is no need to tell West that you have something good in clubs. More importantly, you cannot afford to discard a club! South has denied four cards in either major suit and there is a big chance that he holds four clubs. So throw the ♥2 and retain that potentially useful club holding. When declarer plays a fourth round of diamonds, throw another heart. Declarer will finesse the ♣J, cash the ♣A and play another club. If you had thrown a club away, South's last club would now be established and would give him the contract. Since you kept all your clubs, the game will go down. The defenders will score two clubs and three spades.

Which spot cards count as a 'high' discard?

As we mentioned when we looked at signals, there is not much sense in agreeing to discard 'seven or higher' to show strength in a suit. You can only discard the cards that you are dealt. If you decide to throw a diamond from ♦K-Q-4-2, you will have to discard the ♦4. Partner must make allowance for the fact that he can see several of the higher spot cards in his own hand and in the dummy, and he will note that the ♦2 is missing.

The same is true if you have to discard from ♠10-8-7. You throw your lowest spade, the seven, to indicate a lack of interest in the suit. The last thing you want to hear at the end of the deal is, "But, partner, you showed interest in spades."

Sometimes you can avoid such a problem. Instead of trying to encourage diamonds from ♦K-Q-4-2, give a discouraging discard in the other suit that partner might play.

What does it mean if you discard an honor?

Suppose you hold ♠K-Q-J-10-2 and want to make a discard to indicate your strong holding. Which card will you throw? You should throw the king. By convention, the discard of an honor suggests the honor below and denies the honor above.

Suppose dummy holds ♦A-Q-4 and you have ♦K-J-10-9-3 sitting over it. You should discard the ♦J. This promises the ♦10 and, in this case, suggests that you also hold the ♦K.

Summary

✓ A high discard shows strength in the suit that you throw. It gives partner information but does not necessarily request a switch to that suit. A low discard suggests lack of interest in the suit.

✓ When you wish to show strength in a suit, signal with the highest card that you can afford. From A-10-6-3, signal with the ten if it can be spared, rather than the six.

✓ When you discard an honor, you suggest the honor below it and some sort of sequence. From Q-J-10-9-2 you might discard the queen; from A-J-10-9-3 you might discard the jack.

CHOOSING A HELPFUL DISCARD

NOW TRY THESE...

1.

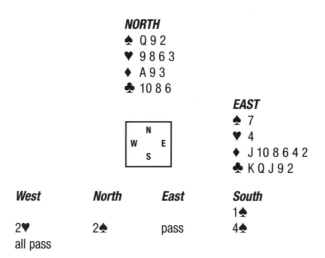

NORTH
♠ Q 9 2
♥ 9 8 6 3
♦ A 9 3
♣ 10 8 6

EAST
♠ 7
♥ 4
♦ J 10 8 6 4 2
♣ K Q J 9 2

West	North	East	South
			1♠
2♥	2♠	pass	4♠
all pass			

West leads the ♥A and continues with the ♥K. Sitting East, how will you defend?

2.

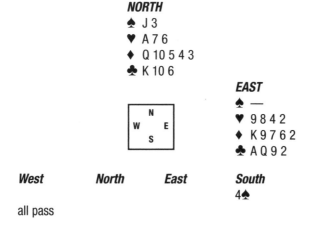

NORTH
♠ J 3
♥ A 7 6
♦ Q 10 5 4 3
♣ K 10 6

EAST
♠ —
♥ 9 8 4 2
♦ K 9 7 6 2
♣ A Q 9 2

West	North	East	South
			4♠
all pass			

West leads the ♥Q against South's spade game. Declarer wins with dummy's ♥A and leads the ♠J. What discard will you make?

ANSWERS

1.

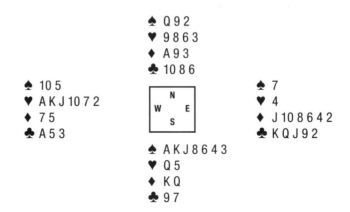

West leads the ♥A and then the ♥K. Sitting East, you should discard the ♣K to show a solid honor holding. Your partner will then switch to ace and another club, defeating the game. If instead you throw a low diamond, West may continue with a third round of hearts. Declarer will then be able to discard a club loser on the third round of diamonds.

2.

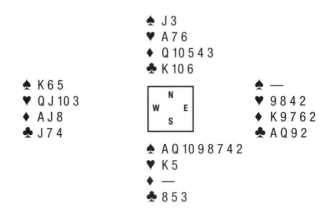

West leads the ♥Q against 4♠. Declarer wins with dummy's ♥A and leads the ♠J. What discard will you make? Are you tempted to throw the ♣9, to show your strength there? You cannot afford this card! When West wins with the ♠K and switches to the ♣J, this will be covered by the king and ace. Declarer will then score a club trick from the ♣10 and the ♣8. Discard a red card instead and declarer will lose one spade and three clubs.

COUNTING DECLARER'S TRICKS

 Facts do not cease to exist because they are ignored.

Aldous Huxley

You may not regard it as good news, but defending well at bridge is mostly a question of hard work. You must gather all the available evidence — from the bidding, the play and partner's signals — and then decide what line of defense will offer you the best chance of beating the contract. The process of gathering evidence is largely a matter of counting. We have already seen how you can count high card points, the shape of the closed hands and the top tricks available to the defenders. In this chapter we will look at counting declarer's tricks and how this can help you to decide how to defend.

What if declarer has enough tricks?

Why do you need to count declarer's tricks? One important reason is that if declarer has enough top tricks available to make the contract, you know you must score immediately whatever defensive tricks you can. It will be a waste of time merely to establish an extra trick or two for later because declarer will make his contract before you can regain the lead.

Let's see a deal on that theme:

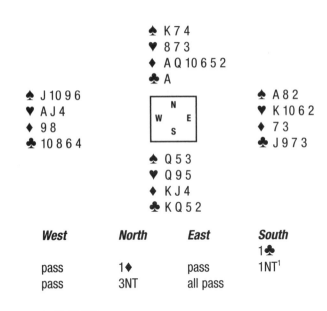

	♠ K 7 4		
	♥ 8 7 3		
	♦ A Q 10 6 5 2		
	♣ A		

♠ J 10 9 6   ♠ A 8 2
♥ A J 4   ♥ K 10 6 2
♦ 9 8   ♦ 7 3
♣ 10 8 6 4   ♣ J 9 7 3

♠ Q 5 3
♥ Q 9 5
♦ K J 4
♣ K Q 5 2

West	**North**	**East**	**South**
			1♣
pass	1♦	pass	1NT¹
pass	3NT	all pass	

1. 12-14 HCP.

Your partner leads the ♠J against 3NT and declarer plays low from dummy. Over to you in the East seat.

When the deal arose at the table, East looked only at the spade suit. Unwilling to let declarer score two tricks with the ♠Q and the ♠K, he played an encouraging ♠8 at Trick 1. The effect of this defense was easy to foresee. Declarer won the first trick with the ♠Q, crossed to the ♣A and returned to his hand with the ♦K. He then cashed the king and queen of clubs, followed by the rest of dummy's diamond suit. Ten tricks!

"What did you have in hearts?" asked East.

"Ace-jack and another," his partner replied.

If East had risen with the ♠A, the defenders could have beaten the contract by taking four heart tricks. How could East know this? He could have little idea of the heart situation, it's true. However, he could be fairly sure that declarer would run at least nine tricks if he was allowed to win the first trick. Six diamond tricks were a near certainty, even if West held the ♦K. The ♣A and a spade trick with the king would bring the total to eight. South's 1NT rebid had indicated 12-14 points, so he must also hold the ♣K or the ♥A. As soon as he gained the lead, he was virtually certain to score nine tricks. The only real chance for the defense was for East to rise with the ♠A and switch to a low heart, hoping for four tricks in that suit. What a shame not to beat the contract when West actually held the ♥A-J-x that was needed!

Counting declarer's tricks can be equally important when defending a suit contract. Take the West cards here:

```
                    ♠ K 10 7 3
                    ♥ Q 2
                    ♦ A 6 2
                    ♣ Q J 9 2
    ♠ —                              ♠ Q J 4
    ♥ K 9 7 4 3          N          ♥ A 10 8
    ♦ Q J 10 5       W     E        ♦ 9 8 7 3
    ♣ K 7 4 3           S          ♣ 8 6 5
                    ♠ A 9 8 6 5 2
                    ♥ J 6 5
                    ♦ K 4
                    ♣ A 10
```

West	North	East	South
	1♣	pass	1♠
pass	2♠	pass	4♠
all pass			

You lead the ♦Q and declarer wins with the ♦K. When he plays the ace and king of trumps, you discard two hearts and partner follows with the ♠4 and the ♠J. Declarer now leads the ♣2 to his ♣10, partner following with the ♣5. How will you defend?

First of all, who do you think holds the ♣A? If your partner held the card, he would surely have played it (to prevent declarer from scoring a singleton ♣K; also to avoid setting up a ruffing finesse against the ace if South held a singleton ♣10). Now count declarer's tricks. You must assume that your partner began with ♠Q-J-4 for the defense to have any chance. This still leaves declarer with five trump tricks. Add the ♦A-K and three club tricks and the total comes to ten. You cannot afford to play the ♦J next. You need to cash two more tricks quickly! The only hope is that East holds the ♥A, so steel yourself to switch to a low heart. If declarer holds the ♥A, you had no chance of beating the contract anyway.

What if declarer does not have enough tricks?

On the two deals that we have seen so far, you could count that declarer had enough tricks to fulfill his contract. You therefore needed to cash some tricks in a hurry. Sometimes you can count that declarer does not yet have enough tricks. In that case you may need to defend differently, making a passive return that will avoid giving a trick away. Look at this deal:

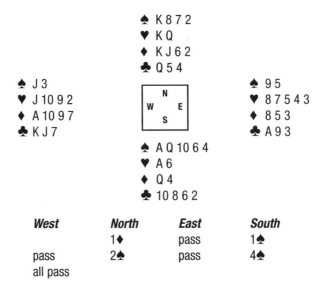

West	North	East	South
	1♦	pass	1♠
pass	2♠	pass	4♠
all pass			

Sitting West, you lead the ♥J against South's spade game. Declarer wins with dummy's ♥K, East following with the ♥3 (a count signal since his attitude is obvious). Declarer draws trumps with the ace and the king, your partner following twice. He then leads a diamond to the queen, East following with the ♦3. How should you defend?

One thing is clear — you should win this trick. Otherwise declarer will lead towards dummy's diamond honors next and you will be in trouble whether or not you take the ace. Next, you need to calculate how you can beat the contract.

Outside the club suit the defenders can score just one trick, the diamond ace. So you need three club tricks to beat the contract. Does that mean you should switch to a club now? No! Even if you make the best switch of the jack of clubs, you will give declarer the contract when he holds ♣10-8-x-x or ♣10-9-x-x. (The jack, the queen and the ace will be played on the first round and declarer can then set up a trick for his ♣10.) There is no need to risk a club switch. Count declarer's tricks. He has five spade tricks and two diamond tricks. In hearts, he clearly holds a doubleton ace — if he held ♥A-x-x, he would have unblocked dummy's remaining heart honor and discarded a club on the third round of hearts, guaranteeing the contract. So declarer has only nine tricks. Exit safely in a red suit and declarer will have to break the clubs himself. Down one!

You could reach the same conclusion by counting the shape of declarer's hand. He has five spades (known), two diamonds (suggested by partner's count signal of the ♦3) and two hearts (deduced because he did not score three heart tricks to discard a club). So, his shape is 5-2-2-4 and you should not be worried about declarer discarding a club on the third round of diamonds.

Summary

✓ There are three things to count when you are defending: points, suit lengths and tricks. You should count declarer's tricks to decide whether you have to defend actively (try to cash tricks) or passively (exit safely to avoid giving away a trick).

✓ Counting declarer's tricks depends on good card reading. You can gather clues from the bidding when players show out of a suit, from partner's count signals and from deductions based on declarer's chosen line of play.

✓ When declarer has enough tricks to make the contract, you need to defend actively. In other words, it will be no use establishing an extra trick somewhere. You must immediately try to cash enough tricks to beat the contract.

✓ When declarer does not have enough tricks to make the contract, it may be unwise to switch to a new suit — perhaps giving declarer an extra trick there. Consider playing safe, exiting in a suit where you know the position and cannot give away a trick.

COUNTING DECLARER'S TRICKS

NOW TRY THESE...

1.

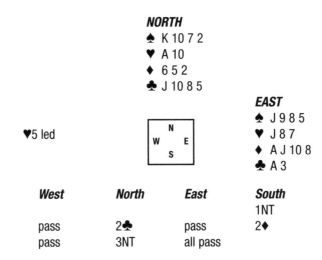

NORTH
♠ K 10 7 2
♥ A 10
♦ 6 5 2
♣ J 10 8 5

♥5 led

EAST
♠ J 9 8 5
♥ J 8 7
♦ A J 10 8
♣ A 3

West	North	East	South
			1NT
pass	2♣	pass	2♦
pass	3NT	all pass	

Your partner leads the ♥5 and dummy's ten is covered by your jack and declarer's queen. At Trick 2, South leads the ♣4 to West's ♣2 and dummy's ♣J. How will you defend? (Yes, North's 3NT was an overbid!)

2.

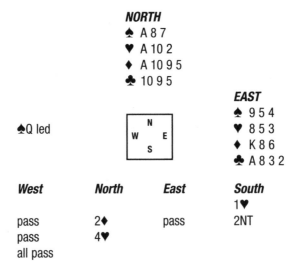

NORTH
♠ A 8 7
♥ A 10 2
♦ A 10 9 5
♣ 10 9 5

♠Q led

EAST
♠ 9 5 4
♥ 8 5 3
♦ K 8 6
♣ A 8 3 2

West	North	East	South
			1♥
pass	2♦	pass	2NT
pass	4♥		
all pass			

Your partner leads the ♠Q and declarer wins with the ♠A in dummy. He draws trumps with the ace, king and queen, West throwing the ♠3 on the third round. Declarer now runs the ♦Q to you. How will you defend?

ANSWERS

1.

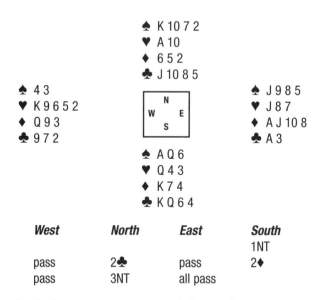

	♠ K 10 7 2	
	♥ A 10	
	♦ 6 5 2	
	♣ J 10 8 5	

West	North	East	South
			1NT
pass	2♣	pass	2♦
pass	3NT	all pass	

Your partner leads the ♥5 against 3NT and dummy's ten is covered by your jack and declarer's queen. At Trick 2, South leads the ♣4 to West's ♣2 and dummy's ♣J. How will you defend?

You must decide whether to clear the heart suit or switch to diamonds, hoping to score four tricks in that suit. How many tricks does declarer have? Look at the club suit first. Your partner's ♣2 is a count signal, showing an odd number of clubs. You can place declarer with a four-card club suit and therefore three tricks in the suit. He has three spade tricks (at most), two hearts and three clubs. That gives him a total of eight tricks. So you have time to clear the heart suit. With the spades breaking badly, declarer has no way to score a ninth trick before you cash two minor-suit aces and three heart tricks.

Suppose instead that West had signaled with the ♣9 on the first round. Since he would signal with his second-best card from something like ♣9-7-6-2, you place him with a doubleton club. Declarer might then have four club tricks, three spades and two hearts for a total of nine. You would switch to the ♦J, hoping that your partner held ♦K-x-x over declarer's ♦Q-x-x and you could score four quick tricks in the suit.

2.

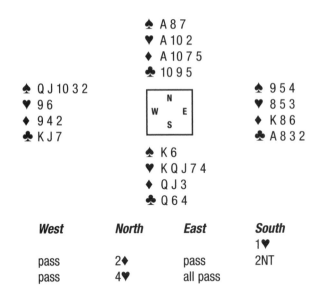

West	North	East	South
			1♥
pass	2♦	pass	2NT
pass	4♥	all pass	

Your partner leads the ♠Q and declarer wins with the ♠A in dummy. You signal with the ♠4, which is an attitude signal, denying the king. (Remember that when dummy's card is the ace, you should ignore the rule to "signal count when your attitude is obvious".)

Declarer draws trumps with the ace, the king and the queen, West throwing the ♠3 on the third round. South now runs the ♦Q to you, West following with the ♦2. How will you defend?

Let's count declarer's tricks. He has five trump tricks and the ace-king of spades. Your partner's count signal of the ♦2 tells you that South holds three diamonds. He can therefore score three tricks from the suit, whether or not he holds the ♦J. That is a total of ten tricks! A spade return cannot possibly be right, because declarer will win with the ♠K and score at least ten tricks. Instead, you must seek three quick tricks in clubs. To clarify the position for your partner, you should play ace and another club immediately.

CHAPTER

KEEPING THE RIGHT CARDS

It's not enough to do our best; sometimes we have to do what is required.

Sir Winston Churchill

A couple of chapters ago, we saw how you can choose a helpful discard to give partner some useful information. We look now at a different aspect of discarding — deciding which cards you need to keep. This is not always easy, since declarer's hand is hidden from view and you may not know which suits you have to guard. This is one of the reasons why you should try to build a complete picture of how the cards lie, by counting points and distribution. There are several general guidelines on keeping the right cards. Let's take a look at them.

Match the length that is in the dummy

When there is a four-card side suit in the dummy, it is easy to see that you may need to keep a four-card potential guard such as J-x-x-x or 10-x-x-x. Suppose you are East here, defending a spade contract:

```
                    ♦ K Q 8 4
   ♦ 10 5          ┌─────────┐          ♦ J 9 7 3
                    └─────────┘
                    ♦ A 6 2
```

Declarer draws trumps and you have to find a discard or two. You will keep all your diamonds because you can see four diamonds in the dummy; you must 'match dummy's length' (sometimes called 'keeping parity with the dummy'). If you started with five diamonds, you could afford to throw one of them because your remaining four cards would still match the length in dummy.

Look back at that diamond diagram. You would need to keep all your diamonds when declarer held just ♦A-6. The same would be true when your partner held the ♦A. Declarer would score tricks with the ♦K and ♦Q but your ♦J would still guard the fourth round of the suit.

Another reason to match dummy's length is to prevent declarer from establishing a trick with a ruff:

```
                    ♣ K 10 6 3
   ♣ 8 4 2         ┌─────────┐          ♣ Q J 9 7
                    └─────────┘
                    ♣ A 5
```

Suppose you discard a club from the East hand, reasoning that you still have a stopper in the suit. Declarer will then be able to cash the ace-king and ruff a club, setting up dummy's ♣10.

This position is similar:

```
                    ♣ A 9 7 3
   ♣ J 6 2         ┌─────────┐          ♣ K Q 10 4
                    └─────────┘
                    ♣ 8 5
```

If you release one of your four clubs, declarer can concede a club trick. Later he will cross to the ♣A and ruff a club, again setting up an extra winner in the suit.

Let's see a full deal where you can beat the contract if you keep the right cards in the East seat:

```
                    ♠ K 6 5 2
                    ♥ A Q J 4
                    ♦ 8 2
                    ♣ Q J 3
   ♠ 9 7                              ♠ J 10 8 3
   ♥ 8 2            ┌─────────┐       ♥ K 10 9 6
   ♦ J 10 9 7 6     │   N     │       ♦ Q 5 3
   ♣ 8 7 5 4        │ W     E │       ♣ 9 2
                    │   S     │
                    └─────────┘
                    ♠ A Q 4
                    ♥ 7 5 3
                    ♦ A K 4
                    ♣ A K 10 6
```

West	North	East	South
			2NT
pass	3♣	pass	3♦
pass	6NT	all pass	

Your partner leads the ♦J against 6NT and South wins with the ♦A. He plays the queen and jack of clubs, continuing with a third round of clubs. What discard will you make from the East hand?

You must match dummy's length in both the major suits and throw a diamond. Look what happens otherwise. If you throw a spade, declarer will score four spade tricks and set up a second heart trick to make the slam. If you throw a heart, declarer will play a heart to the queen and your king and will subsequently score the extra trick he needs with dummy's fourth heart.

Declarer continues with a fourth round of clubs, throwing a diamond from dummy. You must continue your good work on the previous trick by throwing the ♦Q. The slam will then go down. The heart finesse will fail and declarer cannot score an extra trick in either of the majors.

BY THE WAY

Partner's lead of the ♦J helps you here since you know he has a strong diamond holding; that makes it easy to pitch the ♦Q.

Match the length in declarer's hand

Life can be more difficult when the four-card suit that you need to guard is hidden in declarer's hand:

```
                    ♣ A 8 4
   ♣ 10 5          ┌───────┐       ♣ J 9 7 3
                   └───────┘
                    ♣ K Q 6 2
```

It is just as important, obviously, to retain your four clubs in the East seat, matching the length that declarer holds in his own hand. It may be more difficult to realize this, because you cannot see the cards in his hand.

Let's insert that club position into a full deal. Take the East cards and see if you would have kept the right cards to defeat South's slam.

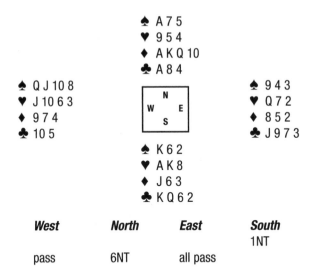

	♠ A 7 5	
	♥ 9 5 4	
	♦ A K Q 10	
	♣ A 8 4	
♠ Q J 10 8		♠ 9 4 3
♥ J 10 6 3		♥ Q 7 2
♦ 9 7 4		♦ 8 5 2
♣ 10 5		♣ J 9 7 3
	♠ K 6 2	
	♥ A K 8	
	♦ J 6 3	
	♣ K Q 6 2	

West	North	East	South
			1NT
pass	6NT	all pass	

Your partner, West, leads the ♠Q. Hoping to give the defenders some discarding problems later in the play, declarer allows the ♠Q to win. West continues with the ♠J, won with the ♠A. Declarer cashes the ♠K and continues with four rounds of diamonds. You must find a discard from ♥Q-7-2 ♣J-9-7-3. What is your choice?

If declarer holds four clubs, a distinct possibility, you need to keep all your clubs. How valuable is your heart holding of Q-7-2? You may be surprised to hear that it is practically worthless! If declarer holds ♥A-K-J, sitting over you, he can finesse the ♥J anyway. If he holds ♥A-K-10, or any lesser holding, your partner's ♥J will guard the suit. So you should discard a heart. A disappointed declarer will score only three club tricks and the slam will go down one.

(If declarer started with ♥A-K-10-x-x on the deal, your ♥Q-x-x would be a stopper, it's true. However, in that case declarer would have won the spade at Trick 1 and played to set up his hearts.)

Do not help declarer to guess right

Suppose you hold a side suit of ♥7-6-5-2. Would you say to yourself, "They're not much use. I'll throw them away"? Usually that would be a sound assessment. Sometimes, though, declarer will have a two-way guess in the suit and you will help him to guess right if you throw away your low cards. That's what might happen on this deal:

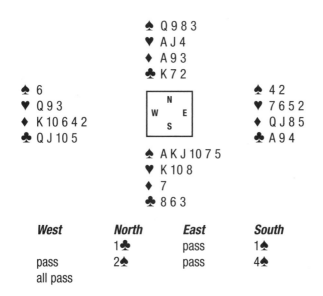

♠ Q 9 8 3
♥ A J 4
♦ A 9 3
♣ K 7 2

♠ 6
♥ Q 9 3
♦ K 10 6 4 2
♣ Q J 10 5

♠ 4 2
♥ 7 6 5 2
♦ Q J 8 5
♣ A 9 4

♠ A K J 10 7 5
♥ K 10 8
♦ 7
♣ 8 6 3

West	North	East	South
	1♣	pass	1♠
pass	2♠	pass	4♠
all pass			

Your partner leads the ♣Q and declarer correctly plays low from dummy. (He knows that you hold the ♣A and if clubs are divided 5-2, your ace will fall on the second round.) Your partner continues clubs and the defenders score three tricks in the suit. Before we consider any problem with discards, what would you play next after winning the ♣A on the third round?

A heart switch is dangerous, because it might help declarer to locate the ♥Q (indeed it would, on the layout that we show). A diamond switch is also dangerous, since it might give away a trick if South held ♦K-10-x. You should therefore switch to a trump, which cannot give a trick away.

Declarer wins the trump switch and runs four more rounds of trumps. How should you discard? Suppose you keep your ♦Q-J-8 and throw two hearts. Declarer may take note of the fact that your partner is keeping all his hearts while you are throwing them away like confetti. He is likely to guess the suit correctly, finessing against your partner's ♥Q.

You should discard a diamond, a heart and then another diamond. If declarer plays his last trump, throwing the ♦9, you will discard the ♦J. You have not helped declarer at all! He will have a difficult guess to make.

Perhaps you are thinking: "Declarer might hold the ♦K-10. In that case my ♦Q-J-8 is a guard against dummy's ♦9." That is true. On such a deal you must use your partner's discards to help you build a picture of the distribution. Here West will throw two diamonds at an early stage, keeping all his hearts. This suggests that he has five diamonds and South has only one.

Summary

✓ As a general guide, you need to match the length that declarer has in a suit. This is easy to do when the length is visible in the dummy — not so easy, sometimes, when the length is in declarer's hand.

✓ When dummy has a holding such as A-9-7-2 in a side suit and you have Q-J-10-8 sitting over the dummy, you may need to keep all four cards. Otherwise declarer can establish an extra trick when he holds K-x-x or K-x (or even x-x-x or x-x).

✓ When declarer may have a two-way finesse for a queen in a suit, be wary of discarding from three or four spot cards. This may make it clear to declarer that your partner holds the missing queen.

✓ You will often need to form a picture of declarer's hand, to decide which cards to keep. Various clues are usually available if you are willing to look for them. The bidding may give you some information and you should look closely at the discards your partner makes.

LEADS, SIGNALS AND DISCARDS

NOW TRY THESE...

1.

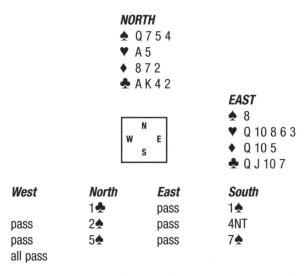

NORTH
♠ Q 7 5 4
♥ A 5
♦ 8 7 2
♣ A K 4 2

EAST
♠ 8
♥ Q 10 8 6 3
♦ Q 10 5
♣ Q J 10 7

West	North	East	South
	1♣	pass	1♠
pass	2♠	pass	4NT
pass	5♠	pass	7♠
all pass			

West leads the ♠2. Declarer wins and plays four more rounds of trumps, West following once more. Which suit or suits can you afford to discard?

2.

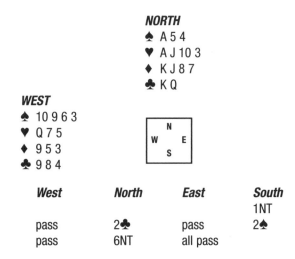

NORTH
♠ A 5 4
♥ A J 10 3
♦ K J 8 7
♣ K Q

WEST
♠ 10 9 6 3
♥ Q 7 5
♦ 9 5 3
♣ 9 8 4

West	North	East	South
			1NT
pass	2♣	pass	2♠
pass	6NT	all pass	

You lead the ♣9 against 6NT, East winning with the ♣A. A club is returned to dummy's ♣Q. Declarer crosses to the ♦A, cashes the ♣J, and continues with the ♦Q and two more rounds of diamonds. What will you discard on the fourth diamond from ♠10-9-6-3 ♥Q-7-5?

ANSWERS

1.

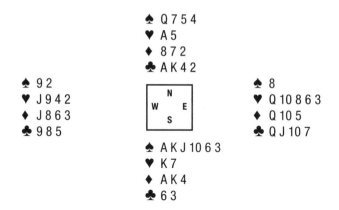

West leads the ♠2 against 7♠. Declarer wins and plays four more trumps. Sitting East, what will you throw?

You can safely throw hearts. If declarer held ♥K-x-x(-x), he would have ruffed his heart losers in dummy. Your diamonds are not worth retaining either. If South has ♦A-K-J, he can finesse anyway. Hold on to those clubs! If you throw one, declarer will play the ♣A-K and ruff a club, setting up a long club for a diamond discard.

2.

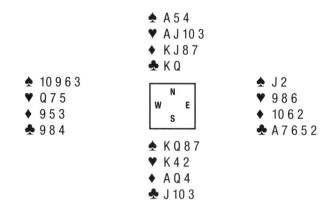

Against 6NT, you lead the ♣9 to the ♣K and East's ♣A. Declarer wins the ♣5 return and plays the ♦A, the ♣J and three more diamond winners. You must find a discard from ♠10-9-6-3 ♥Q-7-5. Declarer's Stayman response tells you he has four spades. You must match his spade length and throw the ♥5. When spades do not break 3-3, declarer may misguess the hearts.

BECOMING A
GREAT DEFENDER

CHAPTER

UNBLOCKING HONORS

♥ Act as if it were impossible to fail.

Dorothea Brande

When you are defending, declarer usually has many more honor cards than you do. As a result, you will want to make full use of the honors you do hold and will be reluctant to waste them. It's an understandable reaction, yes, but retaining an honor can lead to embarrassing consequences. You can block the run of the defenders' main suit; you can also expose yourself to a throw-in. In this chapter we will take a close look at two situations where you should dispose of an honor that might otherwise cause you a problem.

Unblocking a doubleton honor in partner's suit

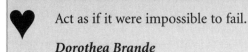

We will start with the common situation where you hold a doubleton honor in the suit that partner has led. Look at this deal:

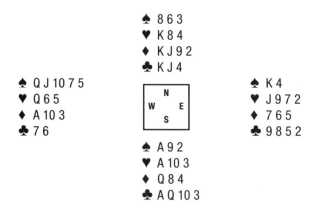

After a 1NT-3NT auction, partner leads the ♠Q. With only two honor cards in your hand, you are not keen to waste either of them. Still, look what will happen if you follow with the ♠4 on the first trick. Declarer will allow the ♠Q to win and partner will lead a second spade to your king. Declarer will allow this to win too and you will have no spade to play! It will make no difference which suit you play next. With his spade stopper intact, declarer will win and set up the diamonds. He will lose just two spades and one diamond, scoring an overtrick.

To avoid this outcome, you must play your ♠K at Trick 1, overtaking partner's ♠Q. Declarer has no counter to this. He will doubtless hold up his ace, but now you can lead the ♠4. Declarer has to win the second or third round of spades. The moment he leads a diamond, your partner will rise with the ace and cash his spade winners, putting the contract down one.

Perhaps you are worried that partner's spades are not quite so strong and the suit lies like this:

	♠ 8 6 3	
♠ Q J 9 7 5		♠ K 4
	♠ A 10 2	

Now when you overtake partner's ♠Q with the ♠K, declarer can win with the ♠A and his ♠10-2 will act as a second stopper in the suit when West wins with the ♦A later. This is true, but you should play your ♠K on the first trick nevertheless. Even when declarer does hold ♠A-10-x, he may decide to hold up the ♠A in case it is you who holds the ♦A (he would then need to exhaust your spade holding). In any case, you will not beat the contract by keeping the ♠K. Declarer will allow it to win on the second round, as we saw before, and make the contract anyway.

Here we see the play in a slightly different guise, in a suit contract:

```
                        ♠ Q J 10 3
                        ♥ A 8 4
                        ♦ K 9
                        ♣ K J 10 4
      ♠ K 5                              ♠ 7 4
      ♥ Q J 10 6 5      ┌─────────┐     ♥ K 2
      ♦ J 6 2           │    N    │     ♦ A 10 8 7 5 3
      ♣ 7 6 3           │  W   E  │     ♣ 9 8 5
                        │    S    │
                        └─────────┘
                        ♠ A 9 8 6 2
                        ♥ 9 7 3
                        ♦ Q 4
                        ♣ A Q 2
```

West	North	East	South
	1♣	pass	1♠
pass	2♠	pass	4♠
all pass			

You are sitting East and partner leads the ♥Q against South's spade game. "Ace, please," says the declarer. Which of your two cards in hearts are you going to play?

Let's see what will happen if you follow with the ♥2, retaining the ♥K. Declarer will run the queen of trumps to your partner's king. He plays another heart and you have to win with the king. Disaster! Since you have no heart to return, you will have to switch to a different suit. Whatever you play next, declarer will win and draw the outstanding trumps. After playing four rounds of clubs, discarding his heart loser, he will surrender a diamond trick and claim the contract.

Once a heart has been led, the defenders deserve to score two heart tricks. You can ensure this by unblocking the ♥K under dummy's ace on the first trick. When West wins with the ♠K, he can then cash the queen and jack of hearts. Your ♦A will then put the game down one.

Unblocking an honor to avoid being endplayed

Declarer cashes an ace in a side suit and you find yourself looking at a doubleton king in the suit. It may be against all natural inclination to throw away your king but we would be failing in our duty if we did not point out that you sometimes need to make such a discard. If instead you hold on to your bare honor, declarer may throw you in, and you may find that you have to give him a trick in a different suit.

Such unblocking plays are difficult, we admit, so feel free to skip to the Summary section! For the brave souls still remaining with us, let's see an example of how you can avoid an endplay by unblocking an honor.

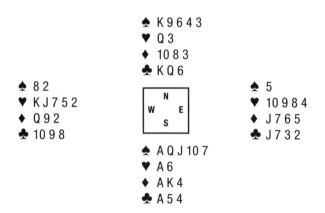

South bids to a small slam in spades and you lead the ♣10. Declarer wins with the ♣A, draws trumps and plays two more club winners. He then cashes the ♦A, leaving these cards still to be played:

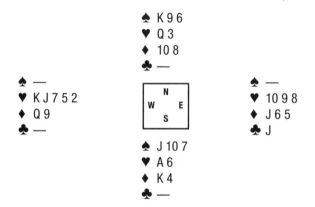

Declarer continues with the ♦K. Which card do you play from your remaining ♦Q-9? Your instinct is telling you to play the ♦9, because the ♦Q is a potential winner. Watch what happens if you do, though. Declarer will throw you in with the singleton ♦Q on the next trick and you will have to lead away from the ♥K on the next trick. Declarer will then score the queen and ace of hearts, making his slam.

It's a difficult play, as we have already said, but you must steel yourself to play the ♦Q under declarer's ♦K. Your partner can then win the third round of diamonds with the ♦J and exit safely in hearts, beating the slam.

How do you know that this is the right play to make? The first pointer is that you *know* declarer will make the slam if you keep the ♦Q. The second pointer is that your partner is almost certain to hold the ♦J. If declarer held ♦A-K-J, he would probably have taken a finesse in the suit.

Summary

✓ When you hold a doubleton honor in the suit that partner has led, you should usually play the honor on the first round. By retaining it, you may block the suit.

✓ When you hold a doubleton honor in one of declarer's suits, be wary of retaining the honor until the second round. When you win a trick with it, you may find that you have no safe card to play.

UNBLOCKING HONORS

NOW TRY THESE...

1.

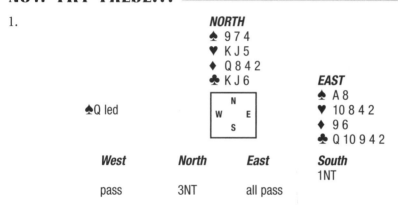

Partner leads the ♠Q against 3NT. How will you defend, sitting East?

2.

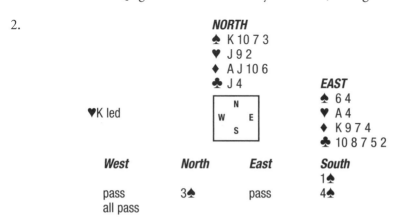

Your partner (West) leads the ♥K against South's game in spades. What is your plan for the defense?

ANSWERS

1.

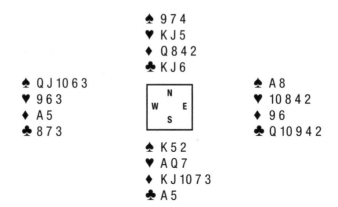

Partner leads the ♠Q against 3NT. How will you defend, sitting East? Let's suppose first that you follow with the ♠8. Whether or not declarer decides to win with the ♠K, the spade suit will be blocked. (If he ducks, you will have to win the next spade with the ace and cannot continue the suit.) Declarer will be able to set up the diamonds and make 3NT easily. Instead you should overtake with the ♠A at Trick 1 and clear the spade suit. When West wins with the ♦A he will cash enough spade tricks to beat the game.

2.

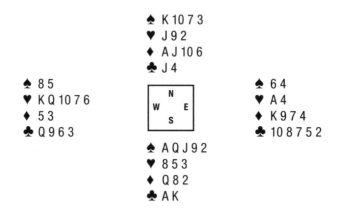

West leads the ♥K against 4♠. You must overtake with the ♥A and return a heart. A heart ruff and an eventual diamond trick defeat the game. If instead you play low at Trick 1, you will block the suit. Declarer will eventually throw a heart on the fourth round of diamonds.

CHAPTER

DESTROYING DECLARER'S COMMUNICATIONS

 Never interrupt your enemy when he is making a mistake.

Napoleon Bonaparte

When you are defending, you have two main objectives in mind. One is to score enough tricks to defeat the contract; the other is to prevent declarer from scoring enough tricks to make the contract. In other words, some of your defensive plays are constructive and some are destructive.

In this chapter we will look at the guerrilla tactics you can adopt to spoil declarer's communications. Take the East cards on the first deal and see if you would have beaten the contract.

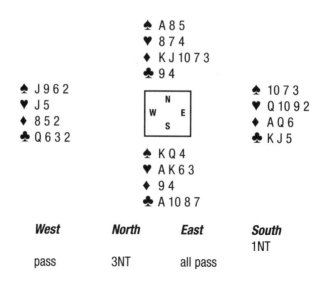

♠ A 8 5
♥ 8 7 4
♦ K J 10 7 3
♣ 9 4

♠ J 9 6 2
♥ J 5
♦ 8 5 2
♣ Q 6 3 2

♠ 10 7 3
♥ Q 10 9 2
♦ A Q 6
♣ K J 5

♠ K Q 4
♥ A K 6 3
♦ 9 4
♣ A 10 8 7

West	North	East	South
			1NT
pass	3NT	all pass	

West leads the ♣2, dummy plays low and declarer wins your ♣10 with the ♣K. He leads the ♦9 from his hand, West following with the ♦2 and dummy playing low. What is your plan for the defense?

It may seem that you can afford to win with the ♦Q and return a spade, hoping that this will drive out dummy's ♠A (your subsequent intention would be to hold up the ♦A, if need be, to kill dummy's diamond suit). This defense will not be good enough. Declarer will win your spade return in his hand, with the queen, and clear the diamond suit while he still has the ♠A in dummy as an entry. He will score three diamond tricks and six top winners in the other suits, making the game.

To kill the diamond suit, you must allow South's ♦9 to win, even though you hold a double stopper in the suit. Declarer continues with a diamond to the ten and you win with the queen. It is not a happy moment for South. He can use his spade entry to dummy to play one more round of diamonds, but will have no way back to cash his winners.

Playing high in second seat to dislodge an entry

We saw, way back in Chapter 4, that it is generally right to play low in the second seat. Most bridge 'rules' have exceptions and we will now see how you can sometimes disrupt declarer's communications by playing high in the second seat. Look at this deal:

```
                        ♠ K
                        ♥ 7 6 3
                        ♦ A J 10 7 6 2
                        ♣ 9 6 4
♠ Q J 10 9 2                              ♠ 7 6 4 3
♥ 9 8 4          ┌─────────┐              ♥ K 10 2
♦ K 5           │    N    │              ♦ Q 9 3
♣ K J 3         │ W     E │              ♣ Q 8 5
                │    S    │
                └─────────┘
                        ♠ A 8 5
                        ♥ A Q J 5
                        ♦ 8 4
                        ♣ A 10 7 2
```

West	North	East	South
			1NT
pass	3NT	all pass	

Sitting West, you lead the ♠Q against 3NT. Declarer wins with the singleton king in dummy and plays a heart to the queen, winning the trick. Although you may not realize it, the key moment of the deal is upon you. How will you defend when declarer leads the ♦4 from his hand?

It may seem natural to play low, but watch what happens if you do. Declarer plays the ♦J from dummy. If East wins with the ♦Q, declarer will score five diamond tricks and make the contract easily. Even if East is smart enough to hold up the ♦Q, the contract will still be made. Declarer will finesse again in hearts and score four hearts, two diamonds and three top tricks in the black suits.

Now see what happens if you rise with the ♦K on the first round of the suit, aiming to dislodge the ♦A from dummy. Whether or not declarer wins the trick with dummy's ace, he can make at most one diamond trick. If he decides to let your ♦K win, and subsequently finesses the ♦J on the second round (hoping that you started with ♦K-Q-x), he will not score any diamond tricks at all!

The same play would be effective if you started with ♦Q-x. Whenever there is a long ace-high suit in an entry-less dummy, consider playing high in the second seat to remove the entry to dummy on the first round.

Return partner's suit or drive out an entry?

Partner leads a suit against 3NT and you win the trick. Will you return his suit? Normally, yes, but sometimes the dummy contains a long suit and your top priority must be to kill an entry before declarer can put it to good use.

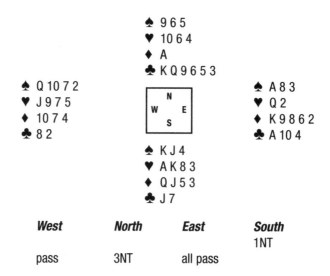

♠ 9 6 5			
♥ 10 6 4			
♦ A			
♣ K Q 9 6 5 3			

♠ Q 10 7 2   ♠ A 8 3
♥ J 9 7 5   ♥ Q 2
♦ 10 7 4   ♦ K 9 8 6 2
♣ 8 2   ♣ A 10 4

♠ K J 4
♥ A K 8 3
♦ Q J 5 3
♣ J 7

West	North	East	South
			1NT
pass	3NT	all pass	

West leads the ♠2 against 3NT and you win with the ♠A. What now?

Suppose you regard returning partner's suit as a civic duty and lead the ♠8 next. Declarer will breathe a sigh of relief, rise with the ♠K and clear the club suit. With the ♦A intact as an entry and only three spade tricks available to the defense, the contract will easily be made.

Civic duties may have to be abandoned when dummy contains such a threatening suit as North's clubs on this deal. Since you hold a club stopper, you know that you can kill dummy's club suit by switching to a diamond at Trick 2. You will then hold up on the first round of clubs and win the second round (partner will give you count, of course). Cut off from the dummy and with only one club trick at his disposal, declarer will go several down.

Let's alter that deal slightly to make the winning defense more difficult… and more spectacular! Once again you are East.

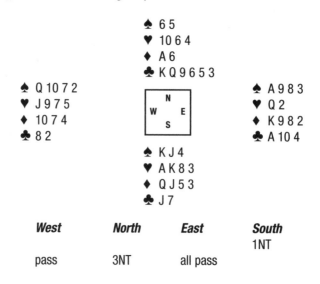

♠ 6 5			
♥ 10 6 4			
♦ A 6			
♣ K Q 9 6 5 3			

♠ Q 10 7 2   ♠ A 9 8 3
♥ J 9 7 5   ♥ Q 2
♦ 10 7 4   ♦ K 9 8 2
♣ 8 2   ♣ A 10 4

♠ K J 4
♥ A K 8 3
♦ Q J 5 3
♣ J 7

West	North	East	South
			1NT
pass	3NT	all pass	

Your partner, West, leads the ♠2 against 3NT. How will you defend?

At the table, East won with the spade ace and, without giving the matter much thought, 'returned partner's suit'. Declarer knew from the fourth-best lead of the ♠2 that spades were breaking 4-4. (Since the two is the lowest card in the suit, there was no way that West could hold a fifth-best card.) Declarer rose with the ♠K and cleared the club suit. The defenders scored three spade tricks and the ♣A, but declarer was able to score five club tricks, bringing his total to nine.

How should you defend on the East cards? You should look with horror at dummy's threatening club suit and wonder how you can prevent declarer from making a bundle of club tricks. Returning a spade and subsequently holding up the ♣A for a round or two will not be good enough; the ♦A will still provide an entry to dummy. The only way to beat the contract is to dislodge the ♦A from dummy.

How about switching to a low diamond? It will not do the job, as the cards lie, because declarer will win with the ♦Q. You need to switch to the ♦K! If declarer wins with dummy's ♦A, you will hold up the ♣A until the second round (exhausting South's clubs) and then switch back to spades. Declarer will have no way to make the contract. Nor will it do declarer any good to duck the ♦K, of course. You would then play another diamond, killing the entry to dummy.

Your sacrifice of your ♦K in a fine cause is such a spectacular play that it has a name of its own. It is called the Merrimac Coup.

BY THE WAY

The name Merrimac Coup is a reference to the USS Merrimac, a ship that was scuttled in Santiago harbor in 1898 in an attempt to blockade the Spanish fleet.

DESTROYING DECLARER'S COMMUNICATIONS

Summary

✓ Even when you hold two stoppers in dummy's long suit, it can be beneficial to hold up on the first round. By winning the second round, you will exhaust an original doubleton holding with declarer and prevent him from playing the suit again when he regains the lead.

✓ When dummy has a long suit such as A-J-10-x-x-x (and no side entry) and you hold a doubleton honor in the second seat, consider playing the honor on the first round. If declarer wins with the ace, his entry to dummy is lost. If he holds up instead, you will score an extra trick in the suit.

✓ When dummy contains a long suit that may provide declarer with several tricks, it is often right to attack any potential entry to the long cards in the suit. When this entry is an ace, you can sometimes force it out by leading an unsupported king from your hand (the Merrimac Coup).

DESTROYING DECLARER'S COMMUNICATIONS

NOW TRY THESE...

1.

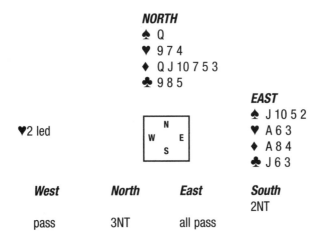

West	North	East	South
			2NT
pass	3NT	all pass	

Partner leads the ♥2 against 3NT. What is your plan for the defense?

2.

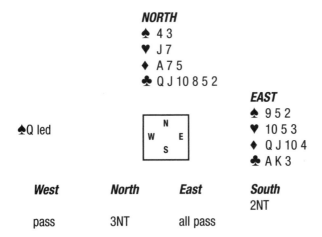

West	North	East	South
			2NT
pass	3NT	all pass	

West leads the ♠Q against 3NT. Declarer ducks and wins the spade continuation with the ♠A. He then leads the ♣9, partner following with the ♣6. What is your plan for the defense?

ANSWERS

1.

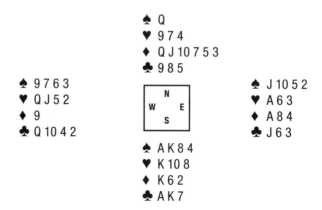

Sitting East, you win the ♥2 lead with the ♥A. If you return a heart, declarer will make the contract easily. He will rise with the ♥K and clear the diamonds. Holding up the ♦A for two rounds will not help you then, because the ♠Q is an entry to dummy. Instead, you should switch to a spade at Trick 2, dislodging the potential entry. You then hold up the ♦A for two rounds and declarer cannot make more than eight tricks.

2.

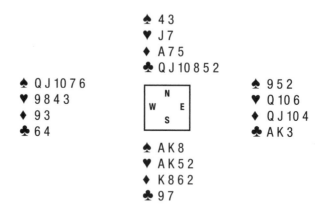

West leads the ♠Q against 3NT. Declarer ducks and wins the spade continuation. He then leads the ♣9. If you win the first round of clubs, declarer will score four club tricks and make the contract easily. Duck the first club and dummy's club suit is dead. The contract cannot then be made.

PROMOTING TRUMP TRICKS

Most people give up just when they're about to achieve success.

H. Ross Perot

After battling through twenty chapters of this book, machete in hand, you may be thinking that defending can be hard work. You are right! It's without a doubt the toughest part of the game, but it is also the most exhilarating when you do it well. We do need a break, though, so in this chapter we will have some fun and look at a topic that involves no hard work at all — promoting extra trump tricks!

Forcing declarer to ruff high

In the most common form of trump promotion, you lead a side suit where both the second player (declarer or dummy) and the third player (your partner) are void. If the second player ruffs low, your partner will overruff. If instead the second player ruffs high, this will promote a trump trick for the defense. Let's see a straightforward example of this defensive technique:

```
                          ♠ Q 10 6 3
                          ♥ 9 8 4
                          ♦ K J 9 2
                          ♣ K 7
   ♠ 9 2                  ┌─────────┐         ♠ A K J 8 4
   ♥ J 7 2                │    N    │         ♥ 6 5
   ♦ 7 6 3                │  W   E  │         ♦ A 10 5
   ♣ 10 8 6 5 2           │    S    │         ♣ Q 9 4
                          └─────────┘
                          ♠ 7 5
                          ♥ A K Q 10 3
                          ♦ Q 8 4
                          ♣ A J 3
```

West	North	East	South
		1♠	2♥
pass	3♥	pass	4♥
all pass			

Your partner (West) leads the ♠9 against South's game in hearts. The ♠10 is played from dummy and you win with the ♠J. What now?

If the opening lead was a singleton, you will score three spade tricks and the ♦A for down one. You play the ♠A at Trick 2, to test the situation, and everyone follows. You can now count just two spade tricks and one diamond trick. Where can a third defensive trick come from?

The answer is that a third round of spades will promote a trump trick for partner if he holds ♥J-x-x or ♥Q-x. When you lead another spade, declarer must decide whether to ruff with a top honor or with the ♥10. If he ruffs with the ace, king or queen, your partner's ♥J will be promoted into the setting trick. If instead declarer ruffs with the ♥10, your partner will overruff with the ♥J. In both cases the contract will be defeated.

That is the basic form of the play, but you must be wary of some possible pitfalls. We will look at a couple of these next.

Cashing winners before attempting a promotion

On the deal in the previous section, declarer was forced to ruff the third round of spades and would go down no matter which trump he chose to play. Sometimes, however, declarer can neatly side-step a trump promotion by discarding a loser on the critical trick. The defenders promote a trump trick, yes, but declarer has lost nothing — swapping one loser for another. A further round of the defenders' suit will cause no problem because dummy will be able to ruff. Let's see a deal that illustrates this situation.

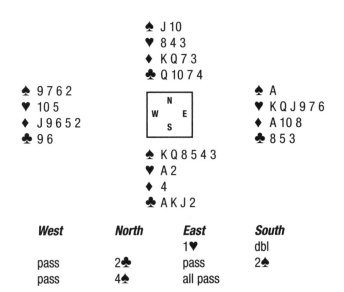

♠ J 10
♥ 8 4 3
♦ K Q 7 3
♣ Q 10 7 4

♠ 9 7 6 2
♥ 10 5
♦ J 9 6 5 2
♣ 9 6

♠ A
♥ K Q J 9 7 6
♦ A 10 8
♣ 8 5 3

♠ K Q 8 5 4 3
♥ A 2
♦ 4
♣ A K J 2

West	North	East	South
		1♥	dbl
pass	2♣	pass	2♠
pass	4♠	all pass	

Again you are sitting East. Partner leads the ♥10 and you overtake with the ♥J, South winning with the ♥A. A trump is played to dummy's jack and your ace. When you play the ♥K, everyone follows. How will you continue the defense?

It may seem obvious to play the ♥Q next, hoping to promote a trump trick for your partner, but see what happens if you do this immediately. Will South ruff high with the ♠K or will he ruff with the ♠8? Neither! He will discard his losing diamond — a 'loser-on-loser' play. The defense will then have three tricks but no chance of a fourth. If you persist with a fourth round of hearts, South will ruff with the ♠8. It makes no difference what West does on this trick. If he overruffs with the ♠9, dummy will overruff in turn with the ♠10. Declarer will then return to his hand to draw all the trumps and claim ten tricks.

To prevent declarer from discarding his singleton diamond when you attempt the promotion, you must cash your ♦A before playing a third round of hearts. West is then assured of the setting trick in trumps, whichever trump South uses to ruff the third round of hearts.

So consider cashing any side-suit winners before attempting a trump promotion. Sometimes this can prevent declarer from discarding a loser as you lead to the key trick.

Be wary of overruffing with a natural trump trick

It is time to look at a second possible pitfall that may arise when you are trying to promote an extra trump trick. This time the focus is on the defender who has the chance to overruff. In such a position, you should always consider whether you may do better not to overruff. By discarding instead, and allowing all your trumps to move up one notch, you may score an extra trump trick. Check out the next deal:

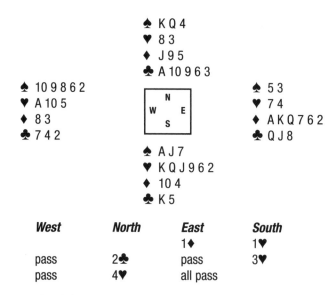

	♠ K Q 4	
	♥ 8 3	
	♦ J 9 5	
	♣ A 10 9 6 3	

West		East
♠ 10 9 8 6 2		♠ 5 3
♥ A 10 5		♥ 7 4
♦ 8 3		♦ A K Q 7 6 2
♣ 7 4 2		♣ Q J 8

	♠ A J 7
	♥ K Q J 9 6 2
	♦ 10 4
	♣ K 5

West	North	East	South
		1♦	1♥
pass	2♣	pass	3♥
pass	4♥	all pass	

Sitting West, you lead the ♦8. Your partner wins with the ♦Q, cashes the ♦A and continues with the ♦K. How will you defend when South ruffs with the ♥K?

Suppose you overruff with the ♥A. Declarer will make the contract easily. He will win your return and draw your last two trumps with the queen and jack, claiming the remaining tricks. Overruffing is an obvious mistake. If you discard instead, you will be left with ♥A-10-5 over South's ♥Q-J-9-6-2. You will be certain to score two trump tricks and defeat the contract.

Suppose next that your trumps were slightly less strong, just ♥A-9-5. It would still be wrong to overruff. Your partner might hold the ♥10, in which case your ♥A-9-5 would be worth two tricks provided you did not overruff.

As a general rule, you should not overruff when there is any chance that you might score more trump tricks by discarding instead.

The uppercut

Now we can look at a completely different, and very enjoyable, way of promoting an extra trump trick. You do this by ruffing with a high trump, usually in the third seat. Declarer (or the dummy) has to overruff with an even higher trump and this may promote a trump trick for your partner. Here is an example of this spectacular play:

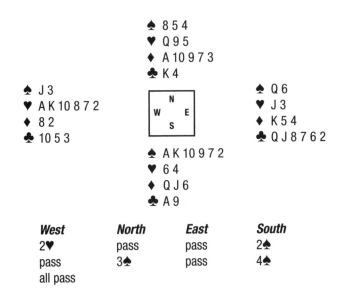

♠ 8 5 4
♥ Q 9 5
♦ A 10 9 7 3
♣ K 4

♠ J 3
♥ A K 10 8 7 2
♦ 8 2
♣ 10 5 3

♠ Q 6
♥ J 3
♦ K 5 4
♣ Q J 8 7 6 2

♠ A K 10 9 7 2
♥ 6 4
♦ Q J 6
♣ A 9

West	North	East	South
2♥	pass	pass	2♠
pass	3♠	pass	4♠
all pass			

West, your partner, plays the ace and king of hearts, everyone following. At Trick 3 he leads another heart, covered by dummy's ♥Q. How will you defend as East?

Suppose you are uninspired and ruff with the ♠6. Declarer will overruff, draw trumps in two rounds and make the contract. He will lose just two heart tricks and a diamond trick. Now try ruffing with the ♠Q instead. This will blast a huge hole in declarer's trump holding! He will have to overruff with the king or ace and your partner's ♠J-3 will be promoted into a trick. The defense will score two hearts, the ♦K and… yes, a trump trick. That is down one.

In a situation where you expect to be overruffed, you should ruff with your highest trump whenever there is a chance that this may promote a trump trick for your partner. The play is known, picturesquely, as an 'uppercut'. It is a fierce blow to the jaw — to declarer's trump holding, in this case.

Summary

✓ There are two basic ways to promote an extra trump trick on defense. You can lead a side suit in a position where your partner has a chance to overruff the player in the second seat. You may also ruff with a high trump (an uppercut) in front of an opponent who can overruff. You hope to knock a hole in the opponent's trump holding.

✓ Before attempting a trump promotion, ask yourself if declarer may be able to discard a singleton loser on the key trick. You may be able to prevent this by cashing a side-suit winner before seeking the trump promotion.

✓ When declarer ruffs with an honor, think twice before overruffing with a higher honor. By discarding instead, you may find that you or your partner can score an extra trump trick. For example, you would usually not overruff the king of trumps with a trump holding of A-10-x.

PROMOTING TRUMP TRICKS

NOW TRY THESE...

1.

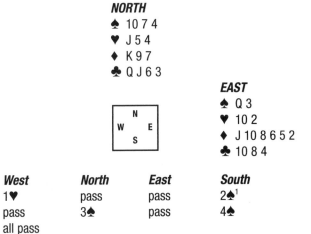

NORTH
♠ 10 7 4
♥ J 5 4
♦ K 9 7
♣ Q J 6 3

EAST
♠ Q 3
♥ 10 2
♦ J 10 8 6 5 2
♣ 10 8 4

West	North	East	South
1♥	pass	pass	2♠[1]
pass	3♣	pass	4♠
all pass			

1. Intermediate.

West leads the ace and king of hearts, declarer following with the ♥3 and the ♥6. How will you defend when West continues with the ♥7?

2.

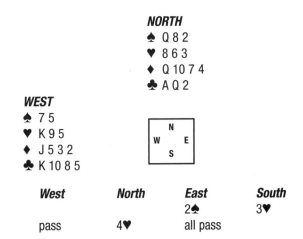

NORTH
♠ Q 8 2
♥ 8 6 3
♦ Q 10 7 4
♣ A Q 2

WEST
♠ 7 5
♥ K 9 5
♦ J 5 3 2
♣ K 10 8 5

West	North	East	South
		2♠	3♥
pass	4♥	all pass	

You lead the ♠7 to East's ♠J. Your partner cashes the ♠A, South following, and continues with the ♠K, South ruffing with the ♥Q. What is your plan for the defense?

3.

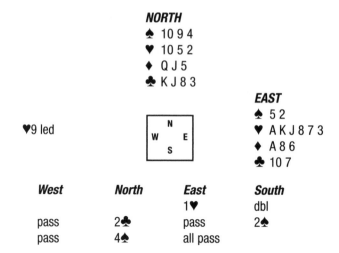

NORTH
♠ 10 9 4
♥ 10 5 2
♦ Q J 5
♣ K J 8 3

♥9 led

EAST
♠ 5 2
♥ A K J 8 7 3
♦ A 8 6
♣ 10 7

West	North	East	South
		1♥	dbl
pass	2♣	pass	2♠
pass	4♠	all pass	

Partner leads the ♥9 and you cash two heart tricks, everyone following. What is your plan for the defense?

4.

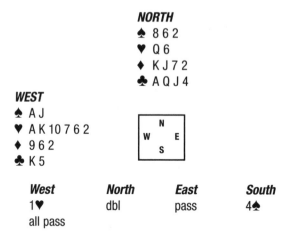

NORTH
♠ 8 6 2
♥ Q 6
♦ K J 7 2
♣ A Q J 4

WEST
♠ A J
♥ A K 10 7 6 2
♦ 9 6 2
♣ K 5

West	North	East	South
1♥	dbl	pass	4♠
all pass			

You lead the ace and king of hearts, partner following with the ♥3 and the ♥5, declarer dropping the ♥J on the second round. What is your plan for the defense?

ANSWERS

1.

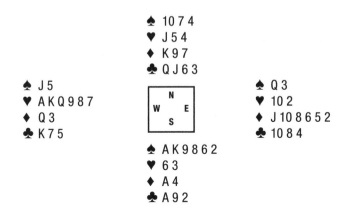

West leads the ace and king of hearts, followed by the ♥7. Do you assume that South must hold the ♥Q and you can ruff low? Not at all! West has led a low heart to tell you to ruff! (If he held ♥A-K-Q-x-x — a five-card suit — instead, he would lead the ♥Q on the third round, telling you that this would win and that you should delay the uppercut until the fourth round of hearts.) In any case, even if South did hold the ♥Q, it could hardly cost to ruff with the ♠Q. So you ruff high and promote a trick for West's ♠J. Declarer cannot avoid the subsequent loss of a club trick and goes down one.

2.

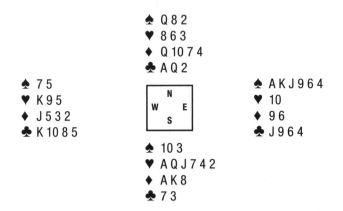

You lead the ♠7 to East's ♠J and he continues with the ace and king of spades, declarer ruffing with the ♥Q. If you overruff with the ♥K, the game will be made. Discard instead and you will score two trump tricks.

3.

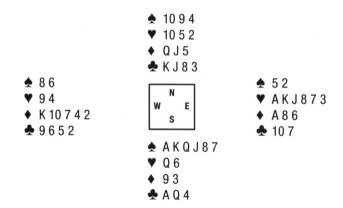

Partner leads the ♥9 against 4♠ and you score the king and ace. Suppose you continue with the ♥J, hoping for a promotion. Declarer will ruff high, draw trumps and discard a diamond loser on the clubs. Game made! Before playing a third heart, you should cash the ♦A. When partner holds ♠Q-x or ♠J-x-x, he will discourage diamonds even when he holds the ♦K. You will then switch back to hearts to promote his trump trick. On the deal shown, West will encourage a diamond continuation! That's down one.

4.

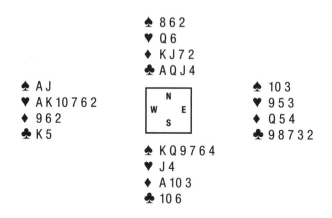

Sitting West, you cash the ♥A-K, partner playing the ♥3 and the ♥5 to show three cards in the suit. Declarer surely holds the ♦A, so you cannot hope for a further side-suit trick. Aiming for a trump promotion, you lead a third heart, giving a ruff-sluff! When you win the ♠K with the ♠A, you play a fourth heart. East uppercuts with the ♠10; declarer has to overruff with the ♠Q and that is down one.

PLAYING A FORCING DEFENSE

Even if you are on the right track, you will get run over if you just sit there.

Will Rogers

What four-card trump holding would you like to have when defending a contract of four spades? Perhaps, after due consideration, you think that ♠A-K-Q-J would be nice. In your dreams! It is much more likely that you will find yourself with something like ♠A-8-7-3. Even a trump holding like this can be a powerful weapon, provided you know how to take advantage of it. The best tactic, by far, is to lead your longest and strongest side suit. Your aim is to force declarer to ruff, thereby weakening his own trump holding. If you can force him to ruff twice from his five-card trump holding, you will then hold more trumps than he does. Declarer will have lost trump control.

This is known as 'playing a forcing defense'. Let's see how it works in practice.

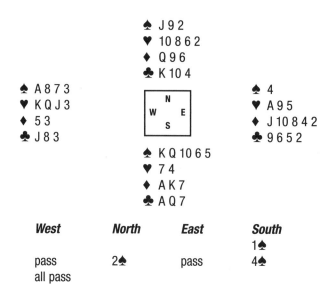

	♠ J 9 2		
	♥ 10 8 6 2		
	♦ Q 9 6		
	♣ K 10 4		

♠ A 8 7 3		♠ 4
♥ K Q J 3		♥ A 9 5
♦ 5 3		♦ J 10 8 4 2
♣ J 8 3		♣ 9 6 5 2

	♠ K Q 10 6 5
	♥ 7 4
	♦ A K 7
	♣ A Q 7

West	North	East	South
			1♠
pass	2♠	pass	4♠
all pass			

Sitting West, with four trumps headed by the ace, you embark upon a forcing defense by leading the ♥K. East encourages with the ♥9 and you continue with a low heart to his ace. When a third round of hearts is returned, declarer has to ruff and is now down to four trumps. When he plays a trump, you win with the ace and play your last heart, forcing declarer to ruff again. He now has two trumps left, while you have three. You will score a second trump trick to defeat the contract.

Even when declarer is playing in a 4-4 fit, rather than a 5-3 fit, he may find that he cannot survive a forcing defense. However, it's a little more complicated than just playing that side suit every time you can. Look at this deal:

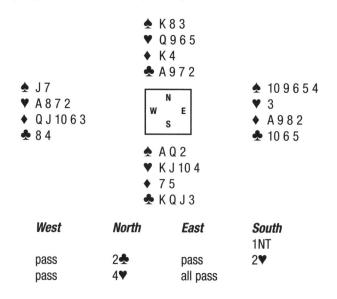

	♠ K 8 3		
	♥ Q 9 6 5		
	♦ K 4		
	♣ A 9 7 2		

♠ J 7		♠ 10 9 6 5 4
♥ A 8 7 2		♥ 3
♦ Q J 10 6 3		♦ A 9 8 2
♣ 8 4		♣ 10 6 5

	♠ A Q 2
	♥ K J 10 4
	♦ 7 5
	♣ K Q J 3

West	North	East	South
			1NT
pass	2♣	pass	2♥
pass	4♥	all pass	

Sitting West, you lead the ♦Q, covered by the king and ace. You win the diamond return and continue with a third round of diamonds, even though this may concede a ruff-sluff. Let's say that declarer ruffs in the dummy and discards from his own hand. How will you defend when declarer continues with a trump to his king?

If you take your ace of trumps now, or on the next round, declarer will be able to ruff the next diamond in dummy (in what has become the short-trump hand). He can then draw trumps and claim the contract. *Instead you must take your ace on the round that includes dummy's last trump.* This will be the position after you take your ace:

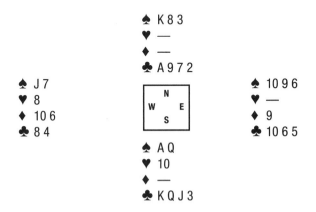

Now you can go back to playing diamonds and *dummy can no longer ruff.* Sooner or later, declarer has to ruff one of your diamond winners and your ♥8 will score a trick.

Summary

✓ When you hold four trumps, consider playing a 'forcing defense'. You attack in your strongest side suit, aiming to force declarer to ruff from his longer trump holding until you have more trumps than he does.

✓ When you hold A-x-x-x in the trump suit, take the ace on the round that includes dummy's last trump. You can then play a further round of your long side suit, forcing declarer to ruff again from the long trump holding.

NOW TRY THESE...

1.

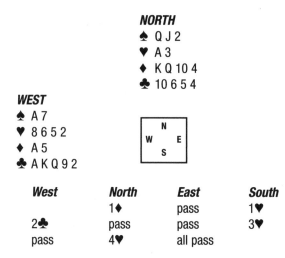

NORTH
♠ Q J 2
♥ A 3
♦ K Q 10 4
♣ 10 6 5 4

WEST
♠ A 7
♥ 8 6 5 2
♦ A 5
♣ A K Q 9 2

West	North	East	South
	1♦	pass	1♥
2♣	pass	pass	3♥
pass	4♥	all pass	

You lead the ♣A, drawing the ♣3 from partner and the ♣8 from South. Declarer ruffs your ♣K continuation and plays the ace and king of trumps, East throwing the ♠3 on the second round. He then leads a small spade from the South hand. What is your plan for the defense?

2.

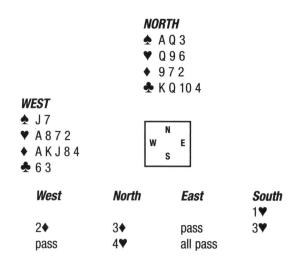

NORTH
♠ A Q 3
♥ Q 9 6
♦ 9 7 2
♣ K Q 10 4

WEST
♠ J 7
♥ A 8 7 2
♦ A K J 8 4
♣ 6 3

West	North	East	South
			1♥
2♦	3♦	pass	3♥
pass	4♥	all pass	

You lead the ♦A and East plays the ♦3, declarer following with the ♦5. What is your plan for the defense?

ANSWERS

1.

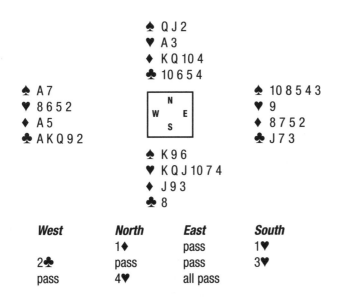

West	North	East	South
	1♦	pass	1♥
2♣	pass	pass	3♥
pass	4♥	all pass	

Sitting West, you lead the ♣A against South's heart game. Partner plays the ♣3 and declarer the ♣8. Even though declarer is likely to hold six trumps, a forcing defense may be successful.

You continue with a second top club and South ruffs. Declarer draws two rounds of trumps, with the ace and king, discovering the 4-1 break. He then plays a low spade from his hand. You must jump in immediately with the ♠A and force South to ruff again with a low club to East's jack.

Declarer now has the same number of trumps as you do in the West seat. He cannot score enough tricks without playing the diamond suit. Whether or not declarer has drawn all your trumps before playing a diamond, you will beat the contract by playing your ♣Q when you take the ♦A. (If declarer has drawn trumps, thereby exhausting his own trumps, your ♣Q will win. If declarer has not drawn trumps, you will force one of his trump honors, promoting a long trump for yourself.)

2

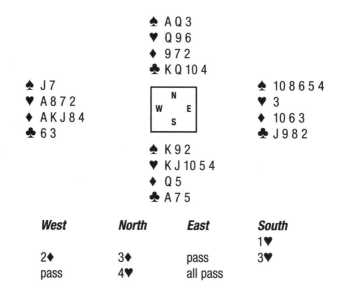

	♠ A Q 3	
	♥ Q 9 6	
	♦ 9 7 2	
	♣ K Q 10 4	

♠ J 7		♠ 10 8 6 5 4
♥ A 8 7 2	N	♥ 3
♦ A K J 8 4	W E	♦ 10 6 3
♣ 6 3	S	♣ J 9 8 2

	♠ K 9 2	
	♥ K J 10 5 4	
	♦ Q 5	
	♣ A 7 5	

West	North	East	South
			1♥
2♦	3♦	pass	3♥
pass	4♥	all pass	

Sitting West, you lead the ♦A against South's heart game, partner playing the ♦3 and declarer the ♦5. How should you continue?

How do you read the diamond situation? If East held a doubleton diamond, he would have played high-low. If he held ♦Q-6-3, he would have encouraged by playing the ♦6. So, the most likely situation is that East holds ♦10-6-3 or ♦Q-3. In both cases it is safe to continue with the ♦K. When you play this card, declarer follows with the ♦Q. You lead the ♦J at Trick 3, forcing declarer to ruff.

When declarer plays trumps, you must hold up your ace for two rounds, making sure to play it on the round that includes dummy's last trump. If instead you win the first or second round of trumps, declarer will be able to ruff a subsequent round of diamonds in dummy (the short-trump hand). Declarer cannot make the contract after this bright start to the defense. If he plays a third round of trumps, you will lead another club, forcing him to ruff with his last trump. If instead he plays his side-suit winners, you will score a ruff with the ♥8.

CHAPTER

CASHING YOUR TRICKS

 People always call it luck when you've acted more sensibly than they have.

Anne Tyler

The opponents bid to 5♣ and you and your partner have three top tricks to cash. Will it be easy to score the tricks that are due you? Not necessarily. You may need to rely on a sound signaling method. Your wish is our command! Here's a special new method to add to your game.

When you are defending a contract at the five-level or higher, you should play this system of opening leads:

The lead of an ace denies the king and asks for an attitude signal

The lead of a king asks for a count signal and promises either the ace or the queen

Suppose you decide to lead from ♠A-K-9-8-2 against a contract such as 5♣. You lead the ♠K. Your partner will then give you a count signal, to tell you whether the second honor can be cashed or will be ruffed. When instead you lead the ace, you deny the king. You may be leading

BY THE WAY

An easy way to remember this is by the sound: Ace for Attitude, King for Count — but it only applies at the five-level or higher.

from ♠A-10-8-2 (not a good idea in general, but sometimes necessary against a very high contract). Partner will give you an encouraging attitude signal if he has the king himself.

Let's see a five-level contract where West needs to know which tricks can be cashed.

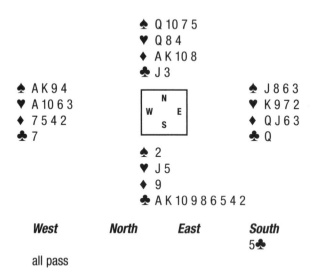

	West	North	East	South
				5♣
	all pass			

Sitting West, you lead the ♠K (king for count). Your partner follows with the ♠8, showing an even number of spades. Since South holds many more clubs than East, the odds are high that East holds four spades rather than two. Furthermore, it is customary to signal with your second-best card when you have four cards. Here, East's ♠8 is consistent with a holding of ♠J-8-6-3. What should you do next?

At Trick 2 you should lead the ♥A. From ♥A-K-x-x you would have switched to the ♥K, so your ♥A switch denies the ♥K. The ace lead requests an attitude signal and East's ♥9 will tell you that he holds the ♥K. You continue with a second round of hearts and the contract is beaten.

If East had discouraged in hearts, you would have tried to cash a second spade trick instead, hoping that South held three spades and East had ♠8-x.

Opening leads that request 'unblock or count'

Now let's look at a method that expert pairs use to determine whether they can cash out (or establish) the suit that they have led against a notrump contract. The idea is that the lead of an ace against a notrump contract asks partner to unblock any honor that is held. If partner has no honor in the suit, he will give a count signal instead.

Imagine the bidding has gone 1NT-3NT and West is on lead with the diamond suit lying like this:

```
                  ♦ 8 4 3
♦ A K J 10 7      ┌──────────┐      ♦ Q 2
                  └──────────┘
                  ♦ 9 6 5
```

West leads the ♦A, requesting an unblock. East duly plays the ♦Q on the first trick and West cashes five diamond tricks to break the contract.

What if the cards lie differently, with East not holding the queen of the suit led?

```
                  ♦ 8 4 3
♦ A K J 10 7      ┌──────────┐      ♦ 9 5 2
                  └──────────┘
                  ♦ Q 6
```

Again West leads the ♦A. This time East follows with the ♦2. This card passes two messages. The first is: "I do not hold the ♦Q." The second is: "I hold an odd number of diamonds." Since there is now an excellent chance that declarer started with a doubleton queen, West will continue with the king. This does indeed drop declarer's queen and once again he scores five tricks in the suit.

If East had been dealt ♦9-2 instead, he would have played the ♦9 at Trick 1. West would then have known that declarer's ♦Q was guarded. Unless he had a quick entry himself (when it might be worth conceding a diamond trick to set up four winners there), West would probably switch to a different suit to avoid giving declarer a trick with the ♦Q.

CASHING YOUR TRICKS

Summary

✓ At the five-level or higher, the opening lead of an ace denies the king and asks for an attitude signal. The opening lead of a king promises the ace or queen and asks for count.

✓ Since (at the five-level or higher) the opening lead of an ace denies the king, partner should encourage only when he holds the king of your suit.

✓ A common agreement is that the lead of an ace (and sometimes a queen) against a notrump contract is a request that partner should unblock any honor or, failing that, give count.

CASHING YOUR TRICKS

NOW TRY THESE...

1.

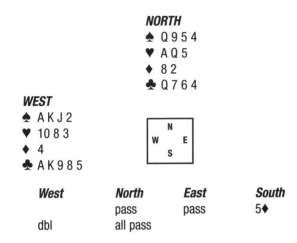

West	North	East	South
	pass	pass	5♦
dbl	all pass		

Sitting West, you lead the ♠K. East plays the ♠8 and South plays the ♠3. How will you continue the defense?

2.

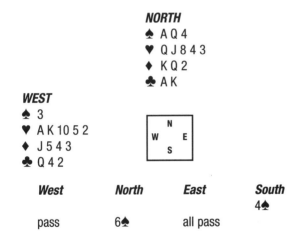

West	North	East	South
			4♠
pass	6♠	all pass	

Sitting West, you lead the ♥K against 6♠. East plays the ♥6 and South plays the ♥9. What next?

ANSWERS

1.

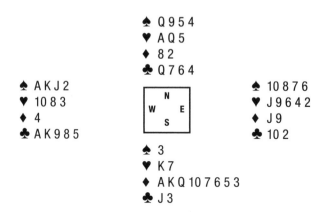

You lead the ♠K against South's 5♦. East plays the ♠8 and declarer plays the ♠3. What now? East has given you a count signal and is likely to hold four spades. You should switch to the ♣K, again asking for a count signal. This time East plays the ♣10 and South plays the ♣J. Since East would not have played the ♣10 from ♣10-3-2, you know that declarer has another club and is trying to fool you. As if he could fool someone playing 'ace for attitude, king for count'! You coolly cash the ♣A, beating the game.

2.

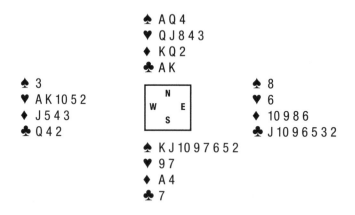

Sitting West, you lead the ♥K against 6♠. East follows with the ♥6 and South plays the ♥9. What next? Your lead of a king requested a count signal. You can see all the lower cards, so partner's ♥6 is his lowest heart. East would not play the ♥6 from ♥7-6, so declarer has another heart! You therefore cash the ♥A and defeat the slam.

CHAPTER

DEFENDING DECEPTIVELY

 No enterprise is more likely to succeed than one concealed from the enemy until it is ripe for execution.

Niccolo Machiavelli

Most declarers will do their best to fool you when they are playing the contract. It is only natural, as defenders, that you and your partner should want to fight back with a few of your own deceptive plays. Is there any scope for doing this? There sure is! In this next-to-last chapter of the book, we will see some of the ways in which it can be done.

Pretending that a finesse has succeeded

There are many situations where you can benefit from persuading declarer that a finesse has succeeded. Look at this slam deal:

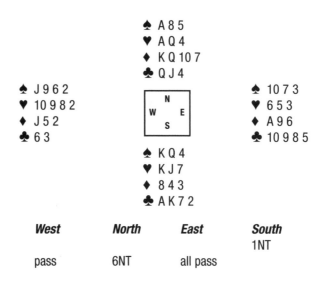

	♠ A 8 5		
	♥ A Q 4		
	♦ K Q 10 7		
	♣ Q J 4		

♠ J 9 6 2   ♠ 10 7 3
♥ 10 9 8 2   ♥ 6 5 3
♦ J 5 2   ♦ A 9 6
♣ 6 3   ♣ 10 9 8 5

♠ K Q 4
♥ K J 7
♦ 8 4 3
♣ A K 7 2

West	North	East	South
			1NT
pass	6NT	all pass	

West, your partner, leads the ♥10 against 6NT and declarer wins with the ♥K. His next move is a diamond to dummy's king. How will you defend in the East seat?

Let's suppose first that you remember some instruction about 'aces are meant to capture kings' and win the trick. Outside diamonds, declarer has ten tricks and no more. He therefore needs two tricks from the diamond suit and will surely finesse dummy's ♦10 when he regains the lead. The finesse will win and the slam will be made.

Next let's suppose that you realize declarer's potential dilemma in diamonds and duck smoothly when he plays a diamond to dummy's king. With eleven tricks now at his disposal, declarer will need one more diamond trick. He will return to his hand in a different suit and lead another diamond towards dummy, West playing low. Not so easy for declarer now, is it? To make the slam, he will have to guess whether to play the ♦Q or the ♦10. Even if he has a high regard for your defensive skills and rates you a strong enough performer to hold up the ♦A on the first round, it will still be a 50-50 guess. West might well hold the ♦A and you might hold the ♦J.

Of course, it is no good to think for a few moments on the first round of diamonds and then hold up the ace. This would give the position away and declarer would surely finesse the ♦10 on the next round. (It would, of course, be very bad ethics to hesitate in the fourth seat when you did not hold the ace.) To stand any chance of beating the slam, you must note the ♦K-Q-10-x when dummy goes down and be prepared to duck smoothly when declarer leads a diamond to the king.

Now let's consider something a bit more difficult. Suppose that *North* is playing 6NT on exactly the same hands. He wins your ♣10 lead in the dummy (South) and leads a diamond to the king. Again you would have to duck smoothly, but this time you could not see what North's diamond holding was. When declarer leads towards a king in the closed hand, he will usually have the queen alongside it. Although you cannot be certain, it will often be right to hold up your ace.

Another reason to pretend that a finesse has succeeded is to persuade declarer to waste an entry in order to repeat the finesse. Consider making such a play when the dummy is short of entries, as on this next deal:

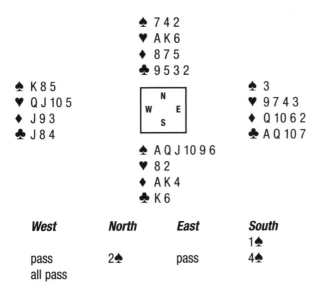

♠ 7 4 2
♥ A K 6
♦ 8 7 5
♣ 9 5 3 2

♠ K 8 5
♥ Q J 10 5
♦ J 9 3
♣ J 8 4

♠ 3
♥ 9 7 4 3
♦ Q 10 6 2
♣ A Q 10 7

♠ A Q J 10 9 6
♥ 8 2
♦ A K 4
♣ K 6

West	North	East	South
			1♠
pass	2♠	pass	4♠
all pass			

Sitting West, you lead the ♥Q against South's spade game. Declarer wins with dummy's ♥A and plays a trump to the queen. What is your plan for the defense?

Perhaps your answer is, "I'm in the middle of a section on pretending that declarer's finesse has succeeded, so I am going to follow smoothly with the ♠5." Correct! Do you see why, though? If instead you win with the ♠K, declarer will use dummy's remaining heart entry to lead towards the ♣K. That will give him ten tricks.

When the ♠Q holds, declarer may well decide to cross to dummy using his last entry (the ♥K) and lead another trump. Enjoy the moment as your partner shows out. With no way back to dummy for a club lead, declarer will lose one spade, one diamond and two clubs.

Why was it fairly safe to hold up your ♠K on that deal? The first reason was that the defenders had no chance of scoring two spade tricks if the ♠K won the first round. If West held ♠K-10-5, it would be slightly dangerous to hold up the king, because this would cost a trick if East began with ♠J-3. Why was it a promising move to hold up the ♠K? Because there was a good chance that declarer would repeat the spade finesse rather than take some more profitable finesse in one of the minor suits.

Concealing your high cards

One of declarer's tasks is to read where the outstanding high cards lie. If you can persuade him that you do not hold a particular card, this may upset his card reading — either of just that suit or of the whole deal. The situation illustrated in the next deal occurs very frequently:

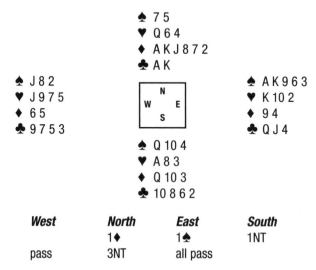

	♠ 7 5	
	♥ Q 6 4	
	♦ A K J 8 7 2	
	♣ A K	
♠ J 8 2		♠ A K 9 6 3
♥ J 9 7 5		♥ K 10 2
♦ 6 5		♦ 9 4
♣ 9 7 5 3		♣ Q J 4
	♠ Q 10 4	
	♥ A 8 3	
	♦ Q 10 3	
	♣ 10 8 6 2	

West	North	East	South
	1♦	1♠	1NT
pass	3NT	all pass	

West leads the ♠2 against 3NT. Sitting East, what is your plan for the defense?

Dummy is a depressing sight. Declarer has eight likely tricks waiting for him in the minor suits, not to mention the ♥A and the spade stopper that he has advertised. What can be done? You must win the first trick with the ♠A, pretending that you do not hold the ♠K. When you return the ♠6 at Trick 2, declarer may guess wrong. He may place West with the ♠K and finesse the ♠10. The defenders will then score five spade tricks to beat the game.

As with many such deceptions, it does not help declarer very much if he has seen such a deceptive play before. He still has to allow for the possibility that you were dealt ♠A-J-9-6-3 and are defending in straightforward fashion.

Play the card you are known to hold

There are several single-suit positions where you can give declarer a tricky guess by playing a card that you are known to hold. In this way, you leave declarer to guess where a different card lies. This is a common position:

```
                     ♠ K962
   ♠ 875            ┌─────────┐         ♠ Q104
                     └─────────┘
                     ♠ AJ3
```

Declarer leads the ♠2 from dummy and takes a successful finesse of the ♠J. What should you do, sitting East, when he continues with the ♠A?

Suppose you 'do what comes naturally' and follow with the ♠10. Declarer will have no guess on the third round. He knows that you hold the ♠Q because the first-round finesse succeeded. When he leads the ♠3 towards dummy, he will rise with the ♠K and score four tricks from the suit.

A better idea is to drop the ♠Q (the card you are known to hold) on the second round. Declarer will then have to guess whether you began with ♠Q-10-4 or ♠Q-4. Since many defenders are not skilful enough to drop the queen on the second round from Q-10-4, declarer may well guess wrong; he will finesse the ♠9 and lose to your ♠10. In any case, the point to remember is that he is bound to get it right if you play the ♠10 on the second round.

If we reduce the cards by one level (always an interesting thing to do), we will see another position where you can give declarer a guess:

```
                     ♣ Q862
   ♣ A75            ┌─────────┐         ♣ J94
                     └─────────┘
                     ♣ K103
```

Declarer leads the ♣2 from dummy and finesses the ♣10, forcing your partner's ace. When declarer regains the lead and plays the ♣K, you must drop the ♣J (the card you are known to hold). Declarer will then have to guess when he leads towards the ♣Q-8 on the third round. If instead you follow thoughtlessly with the ♣9 on the second round, declarer will know that you hold the ♣J and will play for the drop.

Pretending that you can ruff

When you are in a position to score an overruff, declarer may thwart you by ruffing with a high trump. Annoying, yes, but sometimes you can take advantage of this tendency. You can pretend to be poised for an overruff, when you in fact have a card left in the side suit. Declarer avoids the feared overruff by ruffing high and this promotes a trump trick for you or your partner! Let's see this very pleasurable deceptive play in the context of a full deal:

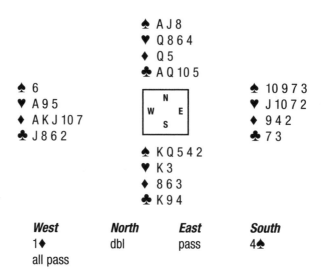

	♠ A J 8	
	♥ Q 8 6 4	
	♦ Q 5	
	♣ A Q 10 5	
♠ 6		♠ 10 9 7 3
♥ A 9 5		♥ J 10 7 2
♦ A K J 10 7		♦ 9 4 2
♣ J 8 6 2		♣ 7 3
	♠ K Q 5 4 2	
	♥ K 3	
	♦ 8 6 3	
	♣ K 9 4	

West	North	East	South
1♦	dbl	pass	4♠
all pass			

Your partner leads the ♦A against South's spade game. How do you assess your defensive prospects from the East seat?

The most likely situation is that West will score two diamond tricks and probably one trick in hearts — not enough to beat the contract, unless you can also score a trump trick. The best idea is to pretend that you hold only two diamonds. You play the ♦9 at Trick 1 and the ♦2 when West cashes his other top diamond.

What will declarer do when West continues with the ♦J? If he places you with a doubleton diamond, he will probably ruff high in the dummy, with the ♠A or the ♠J. This would be the winning play if you did hold only two diamonds and trumps were breaking 3-2. Declarer is about to receive two pieces of bad news, though. First, he will discover that you had three diamonds and he didn't need to ruff high. Second, the trump suit does not break 3-2 and he tumbles to defeat. Savor the moment.

Create a losing option for declarer

Various plays are possible, within the context of a single suit, where you can give declarer a losing option. Suppose you are West here:

	♥ Q 7 2	
♥ 10 9 4		♥ K 3
	♥ A J 8 6 5	

Hoping to pick up the suit without loss, declarer leads the ♥2 to the ♥J. Which card should you play from the West seat? It is easy to see what will happen if you follow with the ♥4. Declarer's only chance of avoiding a loser in the suit is if East started with a doubleton king. He will lead the ♥A next and find that his prayers are answered. What could you have done about it?

Suppose that you drop the ♥9 (or the ♥10) on the first round. Now declarer may imagine that the suit lies like this:

```
                    ♥ Q 7 2
    ♥ 10 9         ┌───────┐         ♥ K 4 3
                    ♥ A J 8 6 5
```

In that case, the winning play will be to return to dummy and lead the ♥Q on the second round. This will catch East's ♥K and pin your remaining middle card, setting up the ♥8 as a third-round winner. If declarer follows this play on the actual layout (where you hold ♥10-9-4), you will score a trick with your ♥10.

As we have observed before, it makes no difference whether you think declarer is likely to guess right or wrong. Unless you are awake enough to drop the ten or nine on the first round, declarer is certain to pick up the suit without loss. You have nothing to lose by dropping a falsecard.

Sometimes you have one winner in declarer's suit and are hoping to make a second trick.

```
                    ♥ A J 7 2
    ♥ 3            ┌───────┐         ♥ K 10 8 4
                    ♥ Q 9 6 5
```

Declarer, who is playing in 4♥, leads a low heart to dummy's jack. If you win with the ♥K, it is easy to see what will happen. The only 4-1 break that declarer can pick up is the one where East holds the outstanding ♥10-8-4. He will therefore play the ♥A next. When West shows out on the second round, declarer will finesse the ♥9 successfully. What can you do about it?

It's the sort of play you might never think of unless you had seen it in a book. You must drop the ♥8 on the first round! Declarer may then conclude that the remaining cards lie like this:

```
                    ♥ A 7 2
    ♥ K 4          ┌───────┐         ♥ 10
                    ♥ Q 9 6
```

In that case he will lead the ♥Q on the second round, hoping to pin your ♥10. Much to his surprise, West will show out on the second round and you will now score two heart tricks.

Whole books have been written on such deceptive plays and we have space for just one more:

```
                    ♥ K 4
    ♥ J 10         ┌───────┐         ♥ A 6 2
                    ♥ Q 9 8 7 5 3
```

Declarer leads a low heart towards dummy and the ten appears from West, covered by dummy's king. If you win with the ace, an alert declarer will reason: "If the ♥10 is a singleton, I cannot pick up East's remaining ♥J-6-2. So I might as well play to drop the ♥J from West."

Now suppose that you make the very clever play of ducking smoothly when dummy's ♥K is played. Declarer will surely finesse the ♥9 on the second round, expecting West to have started with ♥A-10. That's one to remember!

Summary

✓ There are several ways in which you can benefit from pretending that one of declarer's finesses has succeeded. Declarer may repeat the finesse rather than relying on some other chance, or he might waste an entry to repeat the finesse. Finally, if he places the missing high card with your partner, this may affect his reading of the cards in some other suit.

✓ By pretending that you can ruff a side suit, you can sometimes persuade declarer to ruff high. This may promote a trump trick for your side.

✓ Within the context of a single suit, various plays are possible that give declarer a losing option. Some of these involve 'playing the card that you are known to hold'.

✓ By dropping a high spot card on the first round of a suit, you may cause declarer to read you for a short holding and take the wrong view. (For example, drop the nine from 10-9-4 and declarer may try to pin the ten on the next round instead of playing your partner for a doubleton king.)

DEFENDING DECEPTIVELY

NOW TRY THESE...

1.

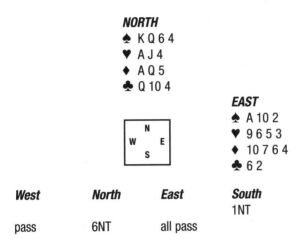

NORTH
♠ K Q 6 4
♥ A J 4
♦ A Q 5
♣ Q 10 4

EAST
♠ A 10 2
♥ 9 6 5 3
♦ 10 7 6 4
♣ 6 2

West	North	East	South
			1NT
pass	6NT	all pass	

West leads the ♣9 against 6NT. Declarer wins with the ace and plays a spade to dummy's king. Will you win or duck smoothly? What is the reason for your decision?

2.

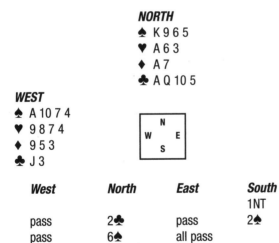

NORTH
♠ K 9 6 5
♥ A 6 3
♦ A 7
♣ A Q 10 5

WEST
♠ A 10 7 4
♥ 9 8 7 4
♦ 9 5 3
♣ J 3

West	North	East	South
			1NT
pass	2♣	pass	2♠
pass	6♠	all pass	

Sitting West you lead the ♥9 against 6♠. Declarer wins with dummy's ♥A, East playing the ♥2, and then leads a trump to the queen. What is your plan for the defense?

DEFENDING DECEPTIVELY

ANSWERS

1.

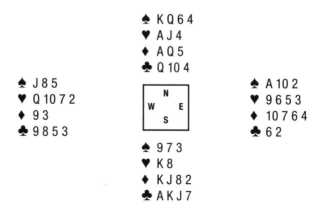

Playing in 6NT, declarer wins the club lead and plays a spade to dummy's king. Suppose you win with the ♠A. Declarer will realize that he needs to finesse dummy's ♥J and will score twelve tricks. Instead you should duck smoothly on the first round of spades. Declarer will then have to guess whether to play a spade to the queen or finesse the ♥J.

2.

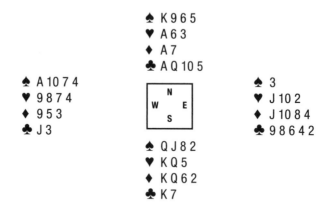

Sitting West, you lead the ♥9 against 6♠. Declarer wins with dummy's ♥A, East playing the ♥2. Declarer then leads a trump to the queen. If you win with the ♠A, declarer may well play the ♠J next and see East show out. He will then finesse dummy's ♠9 for the contract. Duck smoothly instead! It will seem that East is the only defender who can have four trumps. Declarer will surely lead low to dummy's king on the next round. Down one!

PUTTING DECLARER TO A GUESS

Opportunity is missed by most people because it is dressed in overalls and looks like work.

Thomas A. Edison

Given plenty of time, declarer can often combine more than one chance of making his contract. He tests his luck in one suit first. If that suit does not provide the extra trick he needs, he will shrug his shoulders and play for a second chance in another suit. Combining two chances is good business for declarer — and not good at all for the defenders! When you are defending, you must do what you can to force declarer to make a key decision early in the play, rather than allowing him to test another suit first. In this final chapter we will see how you can do this.

Force declarer to guess whether to finesse

When declarer hopes to preserve a finesse as a second option later in the play, you must aim to lead the finesse suit at an early stage. He will then have to guess whether to finesse before he knows how the other suit lies. Let's see this idea in the context of a full deal:

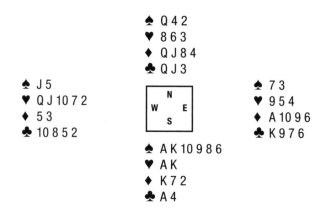

♠ Q 4 2
♥ 8 6 3
♦ Q J 8 4
♣ Q J 3

♠ J 5		♠ 7 3
♥ Q J 10 7 2	N	♥ 9 5 4
♦ 5 3	W E	♦ A 10 9 6
♣ 10 8 5 2	S	♣ K 9 7 6

♠ A K 10 9 8 6
♥ A K
♦ K 7 2
♣ A 4

You are sitting East and partner leads the ♥Q against a contract of 6♠. Declarer wins with the ♥A and draws two rounds of trumps with the ace and king. He continues with a low diamond to dummy's queen. How should you defend?

Declarer's intention is to set up a club discard if diamonds break 3-3 (or if West held ♦A-x, a chance that has now passed). Many Easts would win with the ♦A and return another heart. It is easy to see what would happen after this untaxing defense. Declarer would win with the ♥K and test the diamonds. When the suit failed to divide 3-3, he would take a club finesse. Slam bid, slam made!

A much stronger defense is for East to switch to a club when he wins with the ♦A. Do you see why this is a good idea? It will force declarer to decide what to do in clubs before he knows if the diamonds are breaking 3-3. To create the impression that you hold no honor in clubs, you might switch to the ♣9 rather than a low club. To make the contract now, declarer must play low from his hand, running the club switch to the dummy.

Rest assured that there are many, many declarers who will not choose to do this and will therefore go down. The very fact that you have switched to clubs, with the ♣Q-J visible in the dummy, is likely to convince them that West holds the ♣K. In any case, there is not much advantage in debating whether declarer will guess right or wrong. The point to remember is that he is certain to make the contract if you do not switch to a club.

Force declarer to guess which card to play

Sometimes declarer has set up some discards in the dummy and you know that you must score a certain number of quick tricks to beat the contract. Make declarer guess! Don't just exit passively and allow him to discard his losers. Nor should you cash top cards from your hand if a low card might give declarer a guess in the suit. You are East here:

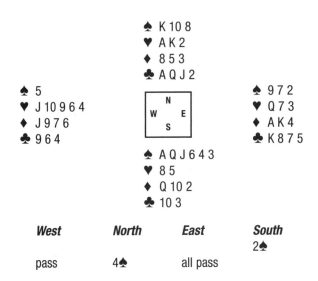

| ♠ K 10 8 |
| ♥ A K 2 |
| ♦ 8 5 3 |
| ♣ A Q J 2 |

♠ 5		♠ 9 7 2
♥ J 10 9 6 4		♥ Q 7 3
♦ J 9 7 6		♦ A K 4
♣ 9 6 4		♣ K 8 7 5

| ♠ A Q J 6 4 3 |
| ♥ 8 5 |
| ♦ Q 10 2 |
| ♣ 10 3 |

West	North	East	South
			2♠
pass	4♠	all pass	

Your partner leads the ♥J against South's game in spades. Declarer wins with dummy's ♥A and draws trumps in three rounds, ending in the South hand. His next move is to run the ♣10 to you. How will you defend?

When declarer regains the lead, he will have more than enough tricks for the contract — six spades, two hearts and three clubs. To beat the game, you therefore need to score three quick diamond tricks. If West holds either ♦Q-x-x or ♦Q-x-x-x, you can afford to play your two top diamonds, followed by the ♦4. Not when the cards lie as in the diagram, though! Declarer will score the ♦Q on the third round.

You must put declarer to a guess by switching to the ♦4! Now declarer has a very difficult guess to make. If you hold the ♦J, whether or not you also hold the ace or king, the winning play will be to insert the ♦10. Only if you hold ♦A-K-x(-x) will it be right to rise with the ♦Q. Declarer is likely to play with the odds and insert the ♦10. Just what you wanted! West will win with the ♦J and return a diamond, putting the game down one.

Make declarer guess whether trumps are breaking

There is another common situation where you can present declarer with a tricky decision. You switch to a card that may be a singleton. Should declarer risk taking a finesse and perhaps suffering a ruff on the return? Or should he rise with the ace and hope that trumps break favorably? The following deal illustrates declarer's dilemma:

```
                    ♠ K 8 3
                    ♥ 10 2
                    ♦ A Q 10 6 5 3
                    ♣ K 2
  ♠ J 10 7 4            N              ♠ 2
  ♥ K Q J 7 4      W         E         ♥ A 9 6 3
  ♦ K 2               S              ♦ 8 7
  ♣ 10 9                                ♣ J 8 7 6 4 3
                    ♠ A Q 9 6 5
                    ♥ 8 5
                    ♦ J 9 4
                    ♣ A Q 5
```

West	North	East	South
			1♠
pass	2♦	pass	2♠
pass	4♠	all pass	

Sitting West, you win the first two tricks with the ♥K and the ♥Q. What next?

South surely holds both black aces for his opening bid, so you can expect to score at most one trick in those suits. With the ♦K in front of dummy's ♦A-Q, it seems that the contract will be made. You have a chance, though. Switch to the ♦2! Look at the situation from declarer's point of view. If the ♦2 is a singleton, he will not want to take a losing finesse and suffer a diamond ruff on the return. Even if he gives you a suspicious look, he may well decide to 'play safe' — rising with the ♦A and attempting to draw trumps. Unlucky! Not only will you turn up with a trump trick, but you will also score the ♦K, which was onside all along.

You can see what would happen if you switched to the ♣10 instead. Declarer would win and draw trumps. When the 4-1 break came to light, he would know that he needed to take the diamond finesse. The finesse would win and the contract would be made.

Summary

✓ Declarer will often wish to test the lie of one suit before deciding what to do in another. By leading the second suit at an early stage, you can sometimes force him to rely on just one chance instead of combining two chances.

✓ When you need to cash quick tricks in a suit, lead the card that may give declarer a guess.

✓ When you have an unexpected trump trick (because the suit is breaking badly), you can sometimes put declarer to a guess in a side suit.

PUTTING DECLARER TO A GUESS

NOW TRY THESE...

1.

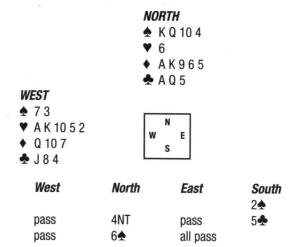

NORTH
- ♠ K Q 10 4
- ♥ 6
- ♦ A K 9 6 5
- ♣ A Q 5

WEST
- ♠ 7 3
- ♥ A K 10 5 2
- ♦ Q 10 7
- ♣ J 8 4

West	North	East	South
			2♣
pass	4NT	pass	5♣
pass	6♠	all pass	

South's 5♣ showed one keycard (which must be the ♠A here). Sitting West, you lead the ♥K against 6♠. How will you continue the defense?

2.

NORTH
- ♠ K 10 7 5 4
- ♥ 6 4
- ♦ Q J 9 5 3
- ♣ A

EAST
- ♠ Q J 6
- ♥ A K 8 5
- ♦ K 2
- ♣ Q 9 4 2

♥J led

West	North	East	South
			1♠
pass	4♣[1]	pass	4♠
all pass			

1. We don't recommend splintering with a singleton ace or king, as it makes it hard for opener to evaluate his hand properly.

West leads the ♥J against the spade game. Sitting East, you win with the ♥K and cash the ♥A, South producing the ♥Q. What now?

ANSWERS

1.

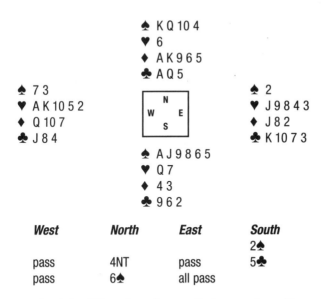

	♠ K Q 10 4	
	♥ 6	
	♦ A K 9 6 5	
	♣ A Q 5	

West	North	East	South
			2♠
pass	4NT	pass	5♣
pass	6♠	all pass	

Sitting West, you lead the ♥K against the small slam and are disappointed to see dummy appear with only one heart. How will you continue the defense?

Suppose you continue passively, switching to a trump or a diamond. Declarer will draw trumps and test the diamond suit. When diamonds break 3-3, he will know that he does not need to take the club finesse. He will discard his two club losers on the long diamonds.

A better defense is to switch to a club at Trick 2. Now declarer must decide whether to finesse in clubs before he knows whether the diamonds are breaking 3-3. On the face of it, the club finesse at 50% is a better chance than finding an even diamond break (36%), so he may well guess wrongly. In any case, you have nothing to lose by forcing declarer to an early decision in the club suit.

2.

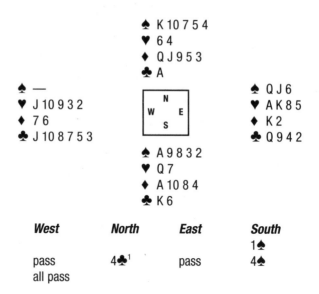

	♠ K 10 7 5 4	
	♥ 6 4	
	♦ Q J 9 5 3	
	♣ A	

West	North	East	South
			1♠
pass	4♣[1]	pass	4♠
all pass			

1. We don't recommend splintering with a singleton ace or king, as it makes it hard for opener to evaluate his hand properly.

West leads the ♥J against the spade game. Sitting East, you win with the ♥K and cash the ♥A, South producing the ♥Q. What now?

South surely holds the ♦A, so it seems that the defenders will score one trump trick and no more side-suit tricks. What will happen, though, if you switch to the ♦2? If declarer fears that the card is a singleton, he will be nervous of playing low, perhaps allowing West to win with the ♦K and deliver a diamond ruff. He may rise with the ♦A and draw trumps, hoping to find spades breaking 2-1. If that happens, you will be happy indeed. Down one!